CORNWALL IN THE AGE OF STEAM

CORNWALL IN THE AGE OF STEAM

A. Guthrie

TABB HOUSE

First published 1994
Tabb House, 7 Church Street, Padstow, Cornwall, PL28 8BG

Copyright © A. Guthrie 1994
ISBN 1 873951 16 7

A catalogue record of this title is available from the British Library

In books lies the soul of the whole Past Time; the articulate audible voice of the Past, when the body and material substance of it has altogether vanished like a dream.

Thomas Carlyle

Typeset by Exe Valley Dataset, Exeter
Printed and bound by Short Run Press, Exeter

PREFACE

Cornwall in its Greatest Days

Since you now seem . . . resolved to make yourself acquainted with the natural curiosities of your country . . . you are entering upon a scene, extremely extensive, I might almost say unbounded, which will always afford something new, and always grow more and more engaging and delightful . . .

Dr John Andrew to Dr William Borlase, February 25th, 1737

THIS essay contains only a little of the author's personal discoveries. It is primarily a concentration for reference of the observations and remarks of some of the many writers, native and outlander, who have examined and recorded the working life of a region that has impressed them, as it has so many in times past. Footnotes have been avoided, not least because so many points have been cross-checked from several sources. Instead, a complete list of references used has been given in the hope that it may help those who wish to make a deeper study.

For geographical and historical reasons Cornwall had been somewhat apart from the mainstream of English affairs since Stuart times. Dickens's friend and collaborator Wilkie Collins could call a holiday tour of the far west in 1850 *Rambles Beyond Railways* with some justice, yet the Duchy had been in the forefront of the great developments of the Industrial Revolution from the eighteenth century. For a time it was the world centre of copper production, backed by an engineering industry of world renown. The number of great figures of the period who took part in, or were influenced by, engineering advances in

Cornwall is legion, and it was a Cornish invention that made steam railroad transport possible.

With the establishment of Mechanics' and Working Men's Institutes in the nineteenth century there were few leading engineers or geologists of the age who did not visit the far west to speak to exacting and intelligent audiences. How seriously mineral discoveries and exploitation in the rest of the world have depleted and deteriorated Cornish life since then is not easy to appreciate, but many areas of the USA, South Africa, Australia and New Zealand bear witness to the great loss of active and able manpower.

It is the purpose of this book to look at that period of Cornish greatness, when the western peninsula was a bustling centre of major industry and, though distinctly and separately Celtic, an important and creative part of Britain. And while the new world was being built the older world continued, so those essential staples, farming and fishing, must be included.

The failure of mining and the rich pilchard industry, the competition of larger steam fishing fleets from England, less quarrying with the increased use of concrete, and the commercial pressure of mechanised farming in the easier Midland and Eastern counties and abroad, has almost totally destroyed the character of the Cornwall of the eighteenth and nineteenth centuries. The railways first and now new roads have created a new industry of tourism, but this has not been compensation of sufficient social advantage, and appears at times to be demeaning and destructive, as in so many 'heritage' buildings dressed up in uncharacteristic colours and trimmings, with sanitized 'theme' displays of plastic Cornish folk, while the real Cornish become outnumbered by settlers, and the landscape vandalised by blights of bungalows.

I am deeply indebted to Roger Penhallurick, Curator at the Royal Cornwall Museum, for reading the MS and giving invaluable criticism, advice and information for the text and guidance for illustrations; to Michael Messenger for details on the railways; to Mr P.S. Butt for his tin mine section, which is available in larger format from the Museum bookstall; to Mr Alan Kittridge for the superb Christmas card of Truro in 1896; and to Miss Angela Broome, Courtney librarian, for her patient and unhesitating supply of source material, however varied the requests. The jacket painting by Terence Cuneo is by courtesy of the directors of Compair Holman, in whose boardroom it hangs, with others illustrating the long history of the Holman family in Cornish mining. I am also grateful for the use of their materials to those named in the List of Illustrations.

A. Guthrie, September, 1993
'Orcadyan' of the Cornish Gorsedd

Contents

List of Illustrations

A New MAP of
CORNWALL,
Drawn from the best
Authorities:
By Thos. Kitchin Geogr.
Engraver to H.R.H. the
Duke of York.

S.T

Borough Towns r
they send to Parlia
Market Towns..
Rectories and Vi
Places where Fair
under the Name t
Tin Mines......

C H A

ISLES
OF
SCILLY

Grim Bishop

Gvan Bishop

Padranthe

White T.
St Martins

Mancar

Tresco

Samson I.
Broad Sd.

Annes

Gough I.

Melledgan

Gorregan

Longit. W. fr. London.

Nanven

Ragged

High

St Marys

Gaints Castle

St Agnes

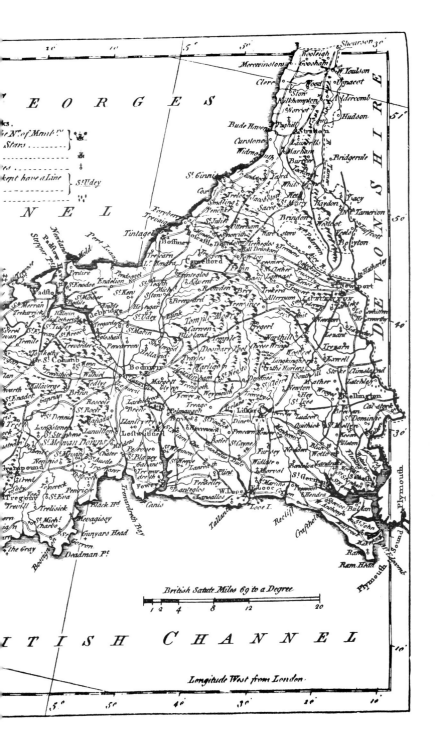

St Ives, 1903

CHAPTER 1

Farming in the Far West

The past is a foreign country; they do things differently there.

L. P. Hartley

In our urban prepackaged society we forget the daily reality of the milking parlour, the yearly necessity of seedtime and harvest. Too often the history of a period or place totally ignores the fundamental daily bread without which the community would not exist. Despite the growing wealth of a developing industrial Britain, and a booming mining Cornwall, 'Give us day by day our daily bread' must too often have been the heartfelt prayer of a great many working men in this County, and further afield.

Organised society starts with farming, and that is where this view of the Duchy will open. Cyrus Redding (1785-1870) says of the region at large that it has 'sterile hills with granite peaks, extended wastes, and districts boasting a fertility surpassed nowhere in the island,' and that applies particularly to West Penwith, which was reputed in a 1935 report to produce two and a half times as much as other south western areas per acre. Redding's note on the climate reinforces this. There is, he says, 'freedom from extremes of heat or cold . . . Even near St Ives . . . more exposed . . . than Penzance, in . . . gardens where there is shelter, the fuchsia may be seen . . . in the extreme west (snow) has rarely been seen to remain on the ground . . . Cabbages are on the table in February, turnips by the end of March; broccoli at Christmas; and green peas the second week in May; the first crop of potatoes is often . . . dug up in April, and the second crop is put in . . . sometimes as late as the middle of July.' It is

1

not surprising, therefore, to find almost forty farms in a parish of only 4,287 acres, including town, mines, woodland and waste, as in St Ives. Many of those farms were settled at a very early date, as the list (illustration 4) shows (and paralleled by many other coastal plain parishes west of the Tamar), but many of the farms are far earlier than their written records; Hendra means old farm, for example.

With four exceptions: Norton of 900 acres in Stratton, Roscarrock in Trigg, Trerice in Pydar and Bodriggan in Powder of 600 or 700 acres each, the size of farms in the County is noted by Worgan as being 'from the barton of three or four hundred acres, down to the cottage holding of three or four acres.' It must be remembered that what are today, or have been recently,

Picking potatoes, Redruth, late nineteenth century

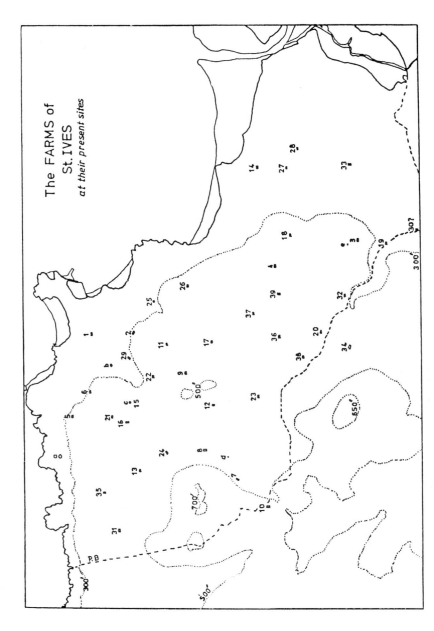

(See key overleaf)

St Ives Parish Farms

With early name, first mention and meaning, from P.A.S. Pool

1	**Ayr**	Arthia, Arthye, 1284. Height + Ia
2	**Bahavella**	Baghevele, 1300. Nook by an apple tree
3	**Beersheba**	Bosaberdu, 1327. Bos aber du - dwelling by dark river mouth?
4	**Boskerris**	Boskeures, 1314. Hedged or enclosed
5	**Burthallan**	Higher, Bosworthalan, 1361. Bos + ?
6	**Burthallan**	Lower
7	**Bussow**	Higher, Bosow, 1284. Dwelling or bushes
8	**Bussow**	Lower
9	**Carnstabba**	Carnestable, 1540. Carn + pers. name Stabba
10	**Chytodden**	Chetodden, Tithe Appt. 1840. House in grassland
11	**Corva**	Corvagh, 1297. A nook
12	**Estover**	sic, T.A. 1840. Eng: necessaries alld. by law
13	**Folly**	sic, T.A. 1840
14	**Gunwyn**	Gonewyn, 1302. White Down
15	**Hellesvean**	Hen Lyns = old court + byghan = small
16	**Hellesveor**	Hellesmur, 1284. Mur = great
17	**Hendra**	Hendre, 1327. Hen dre, old farm
18	**Laity**	Lahitty & Layty, 1200. Leghty, milk house, dairy
19	**Mennor**	Meneath, 1611. Menneth, hill

20 **Nance**	Nans, 1327. Valley
21 **Pednanvounder**	Penvonder, 1298. Pen an vounder, end of land
22 **Penbeagle**	Penbegel, 1259. Pen + begel = tump
23 **Polmanter**	Porthmanter, 1298. Porth + ? = entrance to ?
24 **Rosewall**	Redewall, 1246. Res, ford, ros, heath, moor
25 **Genna**	Tregene, Tregheneu, 1301. Tre + pers. name
26 **Treloyhan**	Trelughion, 1359. Tre + ?
27 **Trenoweth**	Trenewyth, 1324. Higher, new farm
28 **Trenoweth**	Lower ditto
29 **Trenwith**	Treyunwith, 1391. Tre + an wyth, the trees
30 **Treva**	Treyva, 1315. Tre + ?
31 **Trevalgan**	Trevaelgon, 1320. Tre + pers. name Maelyon
32 **Trevarrack**	Trevorek, 1284. Tre + ? marghak = horsemen
33 **Trevethoe**	Trevitho, 1150. Tre + ? bedhow = graves
34 **Trink**	Trefrenk, 1311. Tre + Frenk = Frenchman
35 **Trowan**	Trevowan, 1327. Tref + oghen = oxen
36 **Vorvas**	Gorvos, 1298. ? Higher
37 **Vorvas**	Lower, ditto
38 **Westway**	Westvau, 1567. Incs. fow = cave
39 **Withen**	Le Withen, 1309. Gwedhen = trees

Some farms could be much older than the given date, for example, Hellesvean, which held the remains of an eighth-ninth century house. There are other similar fragments in the area.

single farms, were within the last hundred years 'trevs' with several holdings large and small centred on one farmplace. But, as Worgan found, there were more farms renting at £30 to £50 a year than any other kind. Rents in his day varied from 5s. (shillings) or 25p to 50s. shillings (£2.50) per acre, or even on a farm of less than 150 acres from 5s. to £8 in various parts, dependent on soil, aspect and nearness to markets and sea-sand. The 'Golden Mile' between Penzance and Marazion could rent at £13 per acre. Even the availability of 'town-dung' could enhance a farm's value (*West Briton* May 1st, 1812). Worgan also found that the western farms were very small indeed and very highly rented, so perhaps £5 to £8 per acre might be more realistic for the best farms of the western hundred.

Cottages let for £2 to £4 a year, and their fuel in the west was turf, furze and Welsh coals; in the east it was turf – locally 'vags', peat – locally 'turfs', hedge and coppice wood. For cutting turf a special mattock with a blade set at forty-five degrees, or a mattock with an axe back, a 'biddaxe', or 'biddicks' was used. Peat or turf was cut and stacked on edge to dry in summer, and the turf house was a feature of most cottages. An ash-store to make use of the fertilising value of the fuel when burnt is also often to be found.

In the absence of brick clays, and with timber scarce and in demand for the mines, farm buildings were made of the best material to hand – moorstone, the tough granite surviving as a clitter of boulders on the highlands, or the coarse, thick slates of other areas. Using the natural cubic fracture of granite was often the only mason-work done, except perhaps on the coigns, (cornerstones), and full ashlar, (square masoned stone), seems to come late, sometimes as a facing over a wall of random stone set in cob. Sills and transoms, (the bars over doors and windows), were masoned where they showed, while the rest of the house walls would be random stone pointed with lime mortar, as

would the working buildings. Only in sheltered positions were
the upper storeys, or whole walls, made of cob (coarse clay with
or without straw) and lime-washed for weather protection and
tarred for two or three feet above ground level. Despite the high
winds so frequent in the western peninsula which prompted
many farms to be built with low, almost windowless, backs into
the west or south-west, roofs were of heavily netted thatch
well into the nineteenth century, only slowly being replaced by
Delabole or Welsh slate. As late as 1811 complaints were made in
the press about the excessive number of thatch roofs creating a
fire hazard in Truro. North Devon pantiles seem to have been
used widely on industrial buildings. Stone blocks to hold down
the thatch nets or slate roof edges are found from time to time
round old settlements, and the 'helyer' to repair slate roofs with
'heling stones' was a much needed rural craftsman.

From the middle ages on there was a steady nibbling at the
wasteland, extending farm outfields, and accelerated by miners
and others being granted plots in the wastrel to support themselves. Even so, Worgan quotes Mr Wallis, (secretary to the
Cornish Agricultural Society founded in 1793) saying that about
1800 'nearly a fourth part of the county, from 150,000 to 200,000
acres, consists of unenclosed lands, . . . a scanty pasturage for
a miserable breed of sheep and goats throughout the year;
and about 10,000 acres to the summer pasturage of cattle and
sheep.

'Cornwall seems to be rich in non-Parliamentary enclosures,
carried out by private agreement during the era when elsewhere
Parliamentary enclosure was the method adopted,' says W.E.
Tate. He suggests a probable reason for this in the differences
between the English and Celtic open-field systems: 'in the Celtic
system the division was one between "infield" (cultivated every
year and manured to retain its fertility) and "outfield" cultivated
for a period of years, and then allowed to revert to the waste for

a lengthy and indeterminate period of fallow,' as compared with the English three-field rotation. There were only three early Enclosure Acts, all of waste, at Boconnoc in 1809, Castle Dennis (Castle-an-Dinas, St Columb) and Goss Moor in 1811, and Wendron, Mawgan, Sithney and Helston in 1818; three Acts enclosing common fields came later at Brewenlly in Paul in 1841, Carnhewis (Karnewas) in St Keverne in 1842, and Phillack Towans in 1855. Between 1846 and 1880 the General Act of 1845 saw 18 more enclosures of waste in plots between 30 and 1050 acres.

That many field enclosures were very early, some as far back as the Bronze or Iron Ages, has been shown by many archaelogical finds, and even when they are more recent may show their long standing by the great drop in ground-level over the hedge between the bottom of one field and the top of the next below. In many farms of the coastal plains the soil can be at hedge-top level on one side and ten feet below on the other, feet below the hedge grounders, despite the former practice of barrowing drifted soil from field bottom to top.

Worgan surprisingly says that the county was not a dairying area, and the farming emphasis was certainly on corn. The broadcast-sown corn crops cultivated were wheat, barley, oats and *Avena nuda*, an oat locally called pillas, not grown elsewhere in Britain though known in Brittany. It was usually the final crop in ground which had already grown wheat, oats and potatoes, and was a small yellow grain used for feeding poultry and, mixed with potatoes, for fattening pigs. It was last grown in Sancreed in 1867. The harvested grain stood in stooks (shocks) of 15 or 20 sheaves, and were then built into tall 'arish mows' of two or three hundred sheaves if poor weather threatened, before being carried to the rick or thresher. The rare persistence of this method has been observed in W. Cornwall as late as the 1970s. Tenancy agreements (entered at Michaelmas in the west, and at Lady Day in the east) often provided that no more than two corn crops could be taken from newly broken ground, the second always barley or oats, the ground then to remain for two or three years in ray-grass (locally eaver-grass) with red or yellow clover, and to be fed with sea-sand or lime at each fresh tillage.

Threshing in the lower parts of Cornwall was carried out on 'barn-boards', a wood floor about 7 feet by 4 feet on 10 inch joists, with gaps to let the corn fall through and so suffer less damage. Winnowing in the gale-swept west was over canvases in the open, or between the opposed doors of a special barn, a few of which have survived until recent years. By the start of the nineteenth century the back-breaking task of threshing had very generally been taken over by machines on the larger farms, a few

Hand-cutting corn, 1870

worked by water-power, one noted by Worgan as worked by steam, but mostly by horses. Worgan and other writers describe man-powered threshing machines, but in some parts the use of women beating out wheat on a barrel or inclined board still survived.

As a fertilizer blown-sand was not thought useful, but if dredged up (particularly the coralline sand from the Carrick Roads at the mouth of the Fal) or taken from the shore at ebb-tide and drained of salt water it was regarded as of the best, (see p. 112). For instance, an advertisement for the sale of Penwarne Barton, near Mevagissey, read: 'Most admirably situated for manure ... where town-dung may be procured ... ' and 'sea sand may be brought at a trifling expense.' Another very common fertilizer in the hinterland of the fishing ports was 'mun', a mixture of damaged and decayed pilchards and the blood- and oil-soaked salt left after curing. It was usual for this to be buried in a pile of earth and when fermentation had taken place it was mixed with earth and sand to be spread over the fields. When its effects were beginning to wear off a further dressing of lime extended the fertility for another year or two. Oar-weed was used as a fertilizer when storms brought it in, for early potatoes for instance, but the weed was not cut specially except in the Scillies, and then for other use. 'Beat-ashes' (the thick turf that was burnt after a ley of long standing), were very widely used, mainly for the wheat crop, and this particular practice was frequently debated by agricultural writers around the start of the nineteenth century.

The demand for lime was also met by imported limestone carried as ballast in trading vessels, and burnt near the quaysides, both for soil-dressing and building. A fine example by Harvey's dock in Hayle was destroyed in September 1964, but at Gweek the kiln survives, modified and re-used. Another survives at Pont Pill opposite Fowey, and kiln remains may be traced far up many of the creeks of Cornish rivers where shipping today seems impossible.

Root and other crops included turnips (mainly in East Cornwall) and ruta-baga, the Swedish turnip; flat-poll or drumhead cabbage and broccoli, the latter being shipped to Bristol as early as the start of the nineteenth century. Field peas and beans or carrots were not commonly cultivated, and as so often in northern Europe the potato was the great staple crop.

The native Cornish cattle were a small, raw-boned black breed, still living on the heath and furze of the moors in the early nineteenth century, but they could not readily be fattened. On the good farms and on good soil they had already been superseded by larger cattle, North and South Devons in particular. Worgan, though, was not the only writer of his time to say that Cornwall was not a dairying county, and the meat, milk and milk-products were for local consumption. Tall rubbing-stones set in the middle of fields for cattle to scratch against still survive, but are now getting very rare.

'A large white, long-sided, razor-backed pig was the true Cornish breed', said Worgan, but already in his day it was being crossed with Devon, Suffolk, Leicester and Chinese breeds, and combinations of those breeds. How important the pig was to the poorer community is shown by the comments and illustrations of contemporary writers, and such occasions as Fair Mo at St Ives, a pig fair when fattening was complete for the year. As late as 1859 there were 170 pigs styed within the bounds of Truro.

At the start of the nineteenth century a few of the original small Cornish breed of sheep survived on sand-dune areas, and on the high moors where they were grazed for a month and returned to better pasture to strengthen them, and out again. Mainly there were much improved breeds, but 'the small sheep of Gwithian, Perran Sand and Sennen Green had a peculiarly superior flavour, attributed to their eating a small kind of snail numerous in those parts.' Dr Borlase in his journal noted the same of sheep at Newquay. The two snail species concerned, *Cochlicella acuta* and *Cernuella virgata*, only occur on the coast.

Comparatively few horses were kept only for riding, but were put to the plough as needed, or used to lead a team of oxen. A letter from W. Cornwall in 1826, quoted by Hamilton Jenkin, said: 'In no county does the ox stand in higher estimation for all kinds of work than in Cornwall . . . everywhere to be met with drawing the butt, wain or waggon on the road, and the plough and harrow in the fields. They are shod, or as it is locally termed "cued" .' Cues or ox-plates are still occasionally turned up by the plough in old arable land. Hamilton Jenkin adds that two oxen were reckoned equal to one horse, but when they were sold to the butcher after four or five years' work their flesh was better than those which had not worked. They were slow and needed a man and a boy to work a plough team. Oxen were used at the plough up to the end of the nineteenth century on Bodriggan Barton, near Fowey. Worgan says that the Cornish wooden plough with a straight mould-board was still popular, though many other and newer types were being used, including the

Ploughing with oxen, late nineteenth century

turnwrest plough on hilly ground. Harrows were still the old unimproved heavy wood frames.

'No county affords a greater variety of wheel and other carriages than Cornwall', said Worgan in 1811, when other writers were commenting on the scarcity of wheeled vehicles in Devon, but J.M. Stratton in his *Agricultural Record* said in the entry for 1770 'Wheeled farm vehicles introduced to Devon and Cornwall about this date'. The first dray with wheels was reputed to be that of Salmon Bowden of St Cleer in 1750. Worgan lists waggons, wains, one- and two-horse carts, ox-butts, gurry-butts, slides and sledges, and particularly a light and elegant waggon used for corn and hay, faggot-wood etc., (illustration 8-a, b). 8-c is a three-times enlargement of his 'imperfect sketch' of another hay waggon. The wain (8-d) he found light and useful. The sledge or dray (9-a) was common in the west; the ox-butt, drawn by yoked oxen had a rectangular box on an iron axle fixed in one wheel with the other free; the slide-butt (9-b) holding 3 or 4 wheelbarrow loads, horse or ox-drawn, was used to spread sand, etc. about the fields, and a variation, the gurry-butt (9-c) was also used in the west. The dung-pots (9-f) with a drop-door bottom, speak for themselves, and were carried on pack-saddles, which in hilly country with cliff-backed coves were adapted to a wide range of loads. Finally, the hand-barrow, the gurry, well-known in the pilchard trade, was also used to carry corn to winnowing.

It must be noted that while mining Cornwall was playing its important role in the Industrial Revolution, the landlords and managers of the larger estates were equally aware of the agricultural revolution in England. Books on every aspect of the new farming could be found on their shelves, and applied in practice, while many of the lesser yeomen would have been loth to be left behind.

Farm records and account books are notoriously difficult to

find and too often incomplete, and it is from Worgan that some
guidance must be taken. Cornish farm wages, while mining
flourished, compared well with the English, far from generous
though those were, but deteriorated comparatively as mining
failed and England reached her 'Golden Age of Farming'. When
the mines were busy farmers were often hard pressed to raise the
man-power for harvest. Living-in farm servants were paid £8 8s
(£8.40) to £12 12s (£12.60) a year and their board, and maid-
servants £3 or £4 a year. Hireling labour was paid 9s (45p) to
12s (60p) a week, with a limited supply of corn at well under the
market price. Cornish women with 6d. (2½p) to 8d. (3½p) a day
shared the common miserable lot of their sex in the countryside.

The tenant farmers on rack-rented farms, held for fourteen
years usually, seven or twenty-one years only rarely, and those
on the common three-lives leases, were also liable to tithes.
Rack-rents were those raised to the uttermost, greater than a
tenant might reasonably be expected to pay, while tenancies on
three lives were based on the lifetimes of three named persons,
usually children, and ended when the last one died. Further
names were sometimes added if disaster struck all three at
an early age, but that was the landlord's choice. Tithes were
originally tenth parts, later modified. The Great or Sheaf Tithes
were mostly held by laymen, and were generally valued in the
field and agreed for about harvest time, but where they were
held by rectories were moderate. Small Tithes, on all other
produce, were held by the clergy at 1s. to 1s. 6d. (5p to 7½p) in
the £, and at 2s. 6d. to 3s. 6d. (12½p to 17½p) for rectories.

The course of farming through the century, while broadly
following the same pattern as in England, differs from it inevitably by the existence of a fluctuating mining industry, particularly before 1859 with the completion of railway connection
with England. The varying fortunes of mining could greatly
change the demand for labour and the market for food crops in

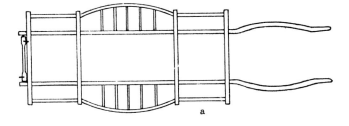

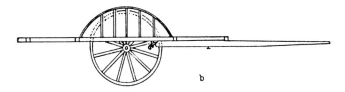

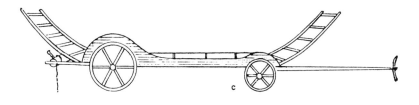

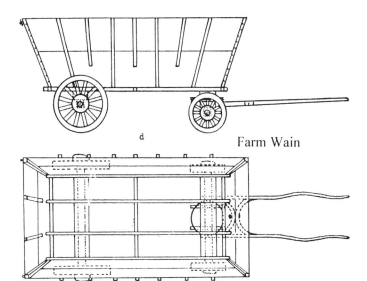

d

Farm Wain

Farm transport, 1811

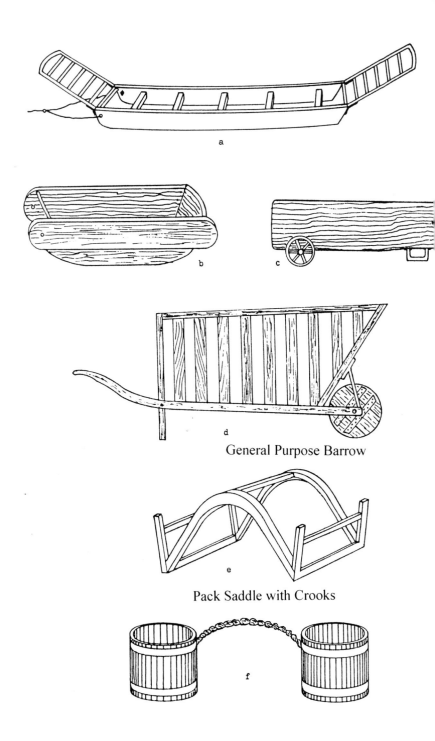

General Purpose Barrow

Pack Saddle with Crooks

any one area, and the potato blight of the late 1840s hit Cornwall as badly as anywhere else, witness the food riots of 1847. No other great changes affected Cornish farms in the hundred years after 1840. The Golden Age of the 1870s in England had no counterpart here, and A.K. Hamilton Jenkins' *Cornwall and its People*, or James Stevens' *A Cornish Farmer's Diary* give us a close picture of the true lot of the small farmer and the hired hand.

From their earliest days the islanders of Scilly scratched a bare subsistence from the sea and small-scale farming, suffering and committing piracy. Though the Spanish, Civil and French Wars brought fortifications and new masters the living standard was minimal. Fishing, pilotage and kelp-making (burning seaweed to obtain potash for soap and glass-making) with smuggling eked out the scanty produce of the little plots scattered about the islands, but by the 1830s Scilly was near famine and disaster, despite £9,000 raised by two Penzance men, a new fish-cellar, new boats and the supply of mackerel and pilchard nets. The Godolphin lease, held for 260 years, was surrendered and was taken by Augustus John Smith, a Hertfordshire landowner, in 1834.

He reorganised the fragmented landholdings, built his own home on Tresco, developed the use of windbreak trees, brought in Guernsey cattle, improved the potato farming, and more importantly, imposed compulsory education in 1850. His nephew Lieutenant T.A. Dorrien Smith, who succeeded him in 1872, noting the success of his uncle's gardens on Tresco, introduced spring flower growing, and the prosperity of the islanders was assured.

CHAPTER 2

Markets, Pleasures and Pastimes

A poor life this if, full of care
We have no time to stand and stare

W.H. Davies

In common with rural England Cornwall was liberally supplied with market towns, and as the business of those places is much alike world-wide it needs little comment. Perhaps it is worth noting, as a comment on the poverty of the small farmer, the insignificant quantities of produce often carried long distances for sale – a pound or two of butter, a dozen or so eggs, a chicken – for the return of a few pence, but that too has been universal.

The farming year did have its high spots, the annual fairs. Directories and gazetteers list up to fifty-six at the start of the Napoleonic war, many in surprisingly small settlements which were then community and market centres, and they continued widely up to the 1860s. Many of the larger centres had several big fairs in the year, and it is among those mainly that any survived into the twentieth century. The fairs were basically trading occasions for the produce of the catchment area, and for the hiring of farm workers, but they were also the sometimes riotous occasion for festivity and relaxation from the grinding harshness of work in field, boat and mine.

As a generalisation it may be said that the further we look back in the nineteenth and eighteenth centuries the less leisure was enjoyed by the ordinary family. Though all work and no play might make Jack a dull boy, that was his station in life and his lot, and questioning it was surprisingly uncommon. To generalise again, the further one looks back the cruder and less sophisticated were the common man's entertainments. To find cock-fighting, badger-, bear- and bull-baiting in the eighteenth century is usual, and they were indulged in by many of the affluent as well as the labouring; all had disappeared, legally, before the end of the nineteenth century, but sadly badger-baiting and dog-fighting still have a few barbarian supporters. In reporting a bull-baiting near Penzance in 1814, when the animal was paraded in ribbons on the day before it was set on by dogs for four or five hours until it collapsed, the correspondent ended 'Such was the scene exhibited in the nineteenth century in the most civilised country of the globe'. What comment can be made on the pit bull terrier at the end of the twentieth? The 'tail-piping' or 'pralling' of dogs (tying on a bullock's horn) and chasing them, popular in Penzance about the same time, seems almost mild in comparison.

The press reported a few dog-fights in the century, the latest organised by showmen at Redruth Fair in 1877, disturbed by the police but not before the dogs were badly mauled, but over the years many more must have escaped unwelcome notice. Equally cruel was the badger-baiting reported as 'The once popular, but now happily almost obsolete practice . . . has been revived at Redruth.' One large badger was caught and kept to fight 'a considerable number of the canine celebrities of the district.'

Cock-fighting, commonplace in the eighteenth century with many towns, like Truro, and inns provided with cockpits (the Ship and Castle, now the Union, Hotel in Penzance for instance) became illegal in 1849, but also had a clandestine survival. A match, attended by a crowd of 100 at St Ive, was dispersed by police as late as March 1875, but again the twentieth century has its reports to show that fighting cocks are not always kept for display alone. Hare coursing and fox hunting were widespread, the former shared by all classes, the latter much more the privilege of the gentry than it is today. Less violent but hardly less cruel was the touring from town to town of a dancing bear, chained and muzzled, taught to shamble to music on its hind legs while its owner took round a hat, or the barrel-organ grinder with his performing monkey.

With such harsh sport with animals widely acceptable man against man could be very bloody, and there was much public violence. Bare-knuckle prize-fighting (the last recorded at Tremenheere, near Ludgvan, stopped by the police) was rarely noted in the press over the century, but the boxing-booth was part of many fairs. The Helston-born world champion Bob Fitzsimmons (1862-1917) fought as a New Zealander, having moved there as a boy.

When coastguard met smuggler, or in quarrels between rival parishes or groups of miners, when religious dissenters refused to pay church dues, in times of food shortage and over political differences, in fact whenever the ordinary public with deep grievances found authority heedless or intransigent riots would flare up. Only too often they were sparked off or made worse by drink, and not infrequently overwhelming the forces of law and order. Even as late as 1896 when Newlyn fishermen rioted against east coast-boats which fished on Sundays, contrary to local custom, naval vessels and soldiers had to be called in to restore order. In 1897 a crowd of two thousand mobbed Sylvanus Trevail when he came to inspect his Headland Hotel in Newquay which had been built on the fenced-off common land promontory.

Public hangings at the County Gaol, Bodmin, were still regarded as entertainment late into the nineteenth century. At the hanging of two brothers in 1840 it was reported that 'every public house, as well as many private houses, was filled to overflowing,' and in the fields opposite the open space in front of the prison where the gallows stood 'there could not have been less than from twenty to twenty-five thousand persons.' In 1854 the West Cornwall Railway brought crowds to Truro to join the walkers, carts, waggons and vans crowding the roads to Bodmin for another hanging. The new gaol had the 'drop' moved from a proposed north siting to the old southern one so that the maximum crowd might view, but in the event an execution in August 1862 was the last to take place in public, and both Cornwall and West Cornwall Railways ran trains to it.

Wrestling was the Cornishman's most popular sport, and part of almost every public festival, governed by strict rules and less violent than some forms of the sport elsewhere. The contestants wore loose canvas jackets on which to take their holds and were barefoot, relying on strength and agility to win. They fought for prizes as large as ten sovereigns, a silver watch and chain or silver cups, with runners-up getting breeches, gloves, gold or silver laced hats or hat ribbons, yet challenges were issued for purses as little as one pound. The county champion also won an elaborate silver-trimmed belt. There was an annual Cornish wrestling match in London, and as miners moved overseas the sport went with them. The first three in a wrestling match in California, reported in the *West Briton* in 1861, were Cornishmen.

The ancient Cornish sport of Hurling, widespread in the eighteenth century and usually part of the parish Saint's Day feast or other special public occasion, was a grand free-for-all, parish against parish, town against country, or even street against street, as in Helston. Sides were unlimited, as many as cared to turn out, with the goals as far apart as geography and custom decreed. The ball was about the size of a cricket ball made of cork, leather or wood cased in silver, while speed, cunning and brute strength kept the game alive until a goal was reached or time ran out. When the game was attacked for its paganism by the Methodists in 1823 Germoe was reported as the only place where it survived, but the newspapers reported it from Newquay, Truro, Probus, St Ives, Tregony, Helston and St Columb during the century. A report from Helston in 1886, however, showed that it had very much faded from past glory. Only at St Columb does the game survive today in its old vigour, with shop windows boarded up and most of the town's young men involved. The game at St Ives is limited now to school children.

Quieter and pleasanter were the contests where worker met worker to prove their skill in their trade, usually for trifling prizes. Competition in ploughing, turnip hoeing, reaping with the scythe, sheaf tossing, walling and hedging all added a little colour to drab lives, and perhaps prestige at Michaelmas if looking for a new master. For pride and pleasure alone, or for prizes, bell-ringing contests were fairly frequent; a trial on St Austell's new eight-bell peal in 1815 offered prizes of £8, £4 and £2 and a silver bell, no small sum for a labourer then.

Sailing matches do not seem to have been very common in the eighteenth or early nineteenth centuries, perhaps because the fishery was such a demanding occupation, but by the mid-century regattas were established in several ports. The Royal Cornwall Regatta at Falmouth in 1846 offered a £20 prize for fishing boats, with Mount's Bay luggers and Cawsand yawls competing, and another for Falmouth pilot boats. At the Marazion and Mount's Bay Regatta in the same year prizes were offered worth over £100 to contestants from Plymouth, Falmouth, Perran, St Mawes, Mousehole, Marazion and Penzance. A women's rowing team from Saltash, having beaten a Portsmouth dockyard crew in 1842, was invited to Le Havre, where the French wouldn't risk defeat, and rowed at many regattas for several years following.

Another trial of strength, which has left its mark in granite blocks riddled with holes like giant woodworm found now built into hedges or abandoned in some derelict yard, was the drilling match. A team of two, holder and striker, or three with two strikers, would drill into the chosen stone for a given time and the team with the deepest hole won. A report from Butte, Montana, in the *West Briton* of November 12th, 1896 told of the world champions, a Cornishman Davey and his mate, driving a steel drill $49\frac{3}{8}$ in (125.5 cm) into granite in 15 minutes, beating the record by $7\frac{3}{8}$ in for a \$500 prize. This was another instance of a Cornish pastime travelling with the miners who had been flooding out of the Duchy to the mining fields of Africa, America and Australia for the two previous decades. Many Cornish inns had skittle or 'kayle' alleys, and a space with an iron pin for quoits with iron rings or horse shoes. Those games also travelled.

From very early times fairs were the high points of pleasure in the working year, and there were many in the eighteenth and much of the nineteenth centuries. The *West Briton* of July 4th, 1862, for instance, lists thirty-two fairs to be held that month in the county. The same issue reports on St Peter's Eve in Penzance with bonfires and torches round the bay, burning tar-barrels, a blazing boat, rockets lighting the town and two fire-balloons sent up. 'All was quiet and . . . no accident' at midnight, the whole affair much the same as it had been twenty years earlier. Midsummer Eve in Penzance was also celebrated with fireworks and bonfires. A Bodmin fair in 1820 had puppet shows, glass blowing, tightrope dancing, giants, dwarfs and jugglers, and those shows and performers made a round of the fairs together with the sellers of fairings and gingerbread, and rogues as well. A Truro fair a few years later ended with seven gambling-table operators and pickpockets moved by the new police to the County Gaol. Pickpockets and conmen are reported again and again through the century. So was the sale of wives, but only the rowdies found that amusing.

The Whitsun Fair in Truro was for pleasure, an occasion for finery in dress, and as much entertainment as was travelling in the county. In 1861, for example, with trainloads arriving from the West Cornwall Railway, there was a fte, a menagerie, a circus, a travelling theatre and other shows, swing boats and 'whirligigs'. We have their descendants still in the fairs that travel the county every summer.

The great majority of the fairs then were primarily markets for cattle and produce, like Bodmin's Garland Ox Fair, with entertainment an added attraction. Stock was judged and prizes given, and the event was a welcome break from the daily grind, an inducement to good husbandry as well, and a traditional part of country life. St Ives' Fair Mo marked the slaughter in the first week of December of the household pigs which had been fattened all summer and were now to be cured for winter fare. Fairings were given by youths to their favoured girls on this occasion. By the 1880s the number of fairs and markets had decreased drastically, probably because better roads and railway transport had made fewer, larger markets more acceptable, and competition was found at the Royal Cornwall Show from its inception in 1793, and such organisations as the Penwith and the Kerrier Agricultural Societies.

Especially to be noticed are three town festivals: the 'Obby 'Oss still flourishing at Padstow, Furry Day revived at Helston and the extinct Bodmin Riding. In Padstow at midnight on April 30th the Hobby Horse 'pare' or gang, having taken supper at the Golden Lion, moved round the town singing the catchy Morning Song, stopping outside various houses. Next day the 'Horse', a great black skirted disc about six feet across resting on his shoulders, with a striped, beaked, tall capped head with horsehair plume and tail, capered round the town with his 'teaser', a man in woman's dress, to the tune of the Morning Song. Occasionally the Horse would dash into the crowd or a house to bump against the women for luck, and the houses which had been serenaded were called at for money for the benefit of Horse and supporters. The dance went on again in the afternoon and there was a fair in the evening. The whole ceremony seems once to have been widespread in Europe, but only at Minehead does a somewhat similar dance survive.

Helston Furry Day, more commonly but incorrectly called Flora Day, falls on May 8th, a festival of St Michael the Archangel, the town's patron saint. Early in the morning young men and girls went out into the country to breakfast, returning at eight o'clock with green boughs, flowers and oak sprigs, led by an old man or woman known as Aunt Mary Moses on a donkey. As the Hal-an-Tow procession reached the town a drum and fife band led it in the now well-known Morning Song, and the church bells were rung. For some time into the nineteenth century the Hal-an-Tow was accompanied by the election of a Mock Mayor of St John's, but the dance was a welcome to summer, dancers in couples moving in at the open front doors of houses and out at the back through the main streets and down to the bowling green. In earlier times the gentry took no part in the morning dance but held their own at noon. On the next day there was a grand hurling match after the beating of the bounds. About the middle of the century the Hal-an-Tow had become an excuse for begging and rowdiness, falling into such ill favour that it had ceased, and after a disreputable revival in 1865 was banned. It was not renewed until 1930. Mock Mayors with their election celebration were commonplace throughout the county, even in hamlets like Halsetown, near St Ives.

The Bodmin Riding was unique to the town, held on the Sunday nearest to July 7th. Beer, brewed and bottled the previous October, was carried round the town accompanied by a drum and fife band and offered to each house with good wishes. The majority who accepted made appropriate payment to the celebration funds. A special Sunday service was followed next day with a procession of everyone who could ride a horse or ass, with the trade guilds, to Bodmin Priory to receive a garland and a decorated pole. All then went to a field west of the town for a day of sports starting with wrestling. On Tuesday there was a bell-ringing contest and more wrestling for big prizes, £10 for first, £5 and £2, and the day ended with a grand ball for servant girls and their followers. That series of events was in 1824, but as at Helston the Riding deteriorated into drinking and rowdiness and was discontinued.

That so many of the old customary celebrations petered out in unruly behaviour was perhaps due to the widening gap between gentry and commoner, but may well have been helped by extensive poverty and the plentiful sources of alcoholic drink. Reports show Bodmin as having 29 public houses and beer shops in 1832, while Penzance in 1838 had 29 public houses and 37 beer shops, and St Ives with a population less than 7,000 at the end of the century had 20 public houses apart from its beer and spirit shops. Even today it has only nine plus one extra in summer. Up to the 1860s it was customary also for public houses to stay open all night on fair days, making trouble almost inevitable.

Many efforts were made to divert the working man from drink by Church, Chapel and Temperance Societies, and by practical alternatives such as Garden Societies to keep men at home. The interpretation of gardening sometimes seems a little odd – Breage Cottage Gardening Society in 1836 gave a £1 prize to the cottager who had brought up the largest family without parish relief, and 10s. (50p) to the second largest, and a 10s. prize to the cottager who had paid in most money to a Benefit Society. However, there was an undertaking for the next year to reward the cottages that were best covered with roses 'providing the dung-pit be not in front of the door.' Food production does not receive a mention. Redruth Cottage Gardening Society, three years later, practically minded, had been distributing seed, but noted that one old lady had successfully grown excellent lettuces but found them quite unsatisfactory whether boiled, stewed, fried or baked! A different approach was made by James Halse in his aim to become an MP for St Ives. He created a village in 1830 where every tenant had enough land with his cottage to make him a voter, and raise enough potatoes to feed his family for a year. The granite cottages were far better than very many of their time and a great attraction; self interest for Halse but an enlightened form of bribery.

Horse racing, trotting races, cricket, football and rugby all have their mention over the nineteenth century but they played a small part in the ordinary man's life compared with today. Some young men from Perran Foundry formed a cricket club in 1847, playing in Sir Charles Lemon's Carclew grounds, but that was unusual, and football never gained much popularity. Only rugby, a fine substitute for hurling, caught the Cornishman's fancy, as it still does.

Guise (pronounced geeze as in geese) dancing in Scilly, Penzance, St Ives and the West Penwith villages, on evenings between Christmas and Twelfth Night, brought out the young disguised in dress of the opposite sex to dance through the streets to whatever music they could make. The costumes were often the discarded best of previous generations, or for the poorer a blackened face or lace veil, and so disguised neighbours' houses were visited, but without offence being given. Guise (pronounced geeze) dancers in many parts of Cornwall also acted a play of St George and the Dragon, the whole affair a relic of a pre-Christian winter festival.

The harvest supper in Cornwall, as elsewhere, marked the end of the farming year, and many other occasions were accompanied by a grand dinner: account day at a mine, the start of any new venture, mine, road, railway, ship launch, any excuse for making life a little less humdrum.

With the coming of the steamship there was cheap transport for outings. From July 1848 when the steam tug *Louisa* started to make excursion trips between Falmouth and Truro there was regular reporting of Sunday Schools, Chapel and Church groups and others sailing particularly on the Fal and Helford rivers, the Tamar, and along both coasts of the county. After August 1852, when the West Cornwall Railway opened, outings by rail continued the widening of horizons for the ordinary citizen; one of the first brought Methodists from west Cornwall to Redruth for Gwennap Pit at Whitsun '53. From the 1880s the safety bicycle offered a further freedom to the better-off working class.

The railway, after the connection to England was made on May 6th, 1859, was the means of opening the county to its future of tourism as mining passed its peak and shrank. It was not long before the first excursion arrived; in June 1860 four hundred travellers from Scotland passed through Truro on their way to Penzance and the Land's End, organised by a Mr Thomas Cook of Leicester. It is to be hoped that they fared better than the traveller on the W.C.R. a year later who wrote to complain of the third class trucks being covered with smelly filth or cow dung and with locked doors. In 1877 Mr Cook was offering hotel coupons, valid at fifteen Cornish hotels at 11s. (55p) for bed and three meals, and a return tour from London to Truro, Penzance, Isles of Scilly, Helston, the Lizard, Kynance and Falmouth for £2 3s. (£2.15p). By 1884 Falmouth had a fleet of twenty-six excursion tugs and steamers, while the G.W.R. offered sleeping cars in 1878 and heated corridor coaches in 1893 from London to Penzance. Tourism was well established, even to the first holiday camp, tented, at Poltesco in the Lizard in 1893.

So far all the pastimes and pleasures mentioned have been

those for the youth and adults of the county. In the eighteenth and much of the nineteenth century childhood for the children of the labouring classes was short and its pleasures few. As has been noted, harsh economic pressure turned a child into a wage earner too soon after infancy, and there was little time or energy for games except for high days and holidays. The pleasures then were unsophisticated: a Sunday School tea treat, May Day dancing round a maypole, sailing cock-boats (a cork hull with a wood-shaving sail), playing marbles with small stones or clay balls, wooden 'joanies' made from broken oars or joist offcuts for girls, bowling iron hoops, playing tipcat (striking a cigar-shaped peg to jump it along, or pitch and toss. Even these might be spoiled, for the *West Briton* in 1824 reported four Helston boys fined 3s, 4d. (16½p) each for playing toss-penny on Sunday, a huge fine for children. Surviving 'cart-wheel' pennies of the early nineteenth century are often badly bruised as a result of that game, which the author has seen still played by gypsy boys in the 1930s. A miserable mayor of Truro in 1838 ordered his constables to confiscate all hoops being used on pavements or roads, which left the young few alternatives.

The sea naturally provided some of the pleasures of the young, swimming or paddling, but generally little boys enjoyed the summer beaches unhampered by swimming costumes, while little girls paddled fully dressed. To the better-off a bathing machine was advertised in Penzance in 1823, for sea-bathing had Royal approval, and two years later one cold and two warm sea-water baths in premises 'built a few years since' in Jennings Street were offered for sale. Similar baths were opened at Charlestown in 1833, but in 1865 a correspondent to the *West Briton* was pointing out that bathing facilities ought to be created at Gyllingvase beach 'near Falmouth'. Eleven years later sea bathing had become so popular that a public meeting at Perranporth decreed exclusive use of the western beach for men up to 9 a.m., and for ladies from 9 a.m. to noon. A few years earlier fifty bathers and boatmen breakfasted on St Clement's Isle, Mousehole, and afterwards swam to Penlee Point, no mean feat. The seaside was well established as a place of pleasure, at least for the better off. There was some opposition from the very strait-laced, complaints to the press of the indecency of bathing being carried on at the quays and river in Truro, and in the docks at Portreath, criticism that certainly hasn't emptied the beaches of Cornwall.

CHAPTER 3

Grist Mills

. . . throughout the length and breadth of the county . . . it has been
suggested there may have been as many as three thousand mills operating at one time or another during the last few centuries.

D.E. Benney

Water-mills

IN a hilly countryside with high rainfall, where corn growing
was the farmers'great preoccupation, and fuel scarce and expensive, water-wheels were an inevitable early solution to power
problems, and they continued to run until long after most of
England had turned to more advanced forms of power. To list
all the grist water mills in the county would be to list every town
many times over, every hamlet and almost every sizeable farm
from the Tamar to Land's End. Not a stream above a trickle
failed to provide power over and over again for milling, mining
and other industries, except perhaps in the uppermost reaches of
the high moors. Many continued to do so, quite widely, well
into the twentieth century. Porcelain clay was ground from china
stone, a special form of granite, by the firm of T. Oliver using a
stair of water-wheel powered mills down a hillside at Tregargus
in the parish of St Stephen near St Austell until 1966.

On farms where the water-wheel could not be built at the
farm place power was sometimes carried by chain or rod drive
for a hundred yards or more from the nearest flow, or a millpool
dammed to provide a head of water from a limited spring. A
great deal of labour and skill was expended on cutting leats to

bring water to the place and height where a mill could be best
sited, often difficult to trace when the mill has been abandoned
for a few years.

John Smeaton, the English engineer who built St Ives harbour, experimented widely to improve the efficiency of wooden
water and wind wheels, and introduced the use of cast iron in
the structure of the wheels in the last half of the eighteenth
century. The millwrights, among the essential skilled artisans of
the countryside, were in many cases, like the enterprising smiths,
to become the first engineers of the steam age, like Smeaton
himself – the first to call himself a Civil Engineer.

Windmills

DESPITE Celia Fiennes' assertion: 'I saw not a windmill all over
Cornwall or Devonshire tho' they have wind and hills enough',
sixty-two grist windmill sites have been traced from field names
and early maps. Nearly all are in coastal parishes, at St Ives on
the north coast, and from St Columb eastwards, and on the
south coast from Marazion to Plymouth with concentrations
round the Fal and Tamar estuaries. Most of the sites must be of
medieval post-mills which have left no trace, but new interest in
the sixteenth and seventeenth centuries created new mills, and
six tower-mill buildings still survive. At least six windmills were
working in the eighteenth century; three remained in the nineteenth century, including one newly built in 1833 *(R.C. Gazette*
March 23rd, 1833). The Buzza Hill windmill in Scilly worked up
to the late nineteenth century, but such canvas-sailed engines,
not unlike the Mediterranean kind, suffered frequently from the
violence of Atlantic gales. Much of the island's grist was still
from rotary hand-querns, usually mounted on a frame to a
convenient height, well into the nineteenth century.

Horse-mills

FARMS lacking water-power, and there were many of quite early foundation, used the horse-mill, or possibly in the eighteenth century ox power, an ancient method also used at some mines. Some of the former survived into the early twentieth century, and the round or octagonal house used, or round platforms, can still be found. Illustrations of mine horse-whims are available but any of horse grist-milling do not seem to have survived.

Tide-mills

Tide-mill, Falmouth, 1831

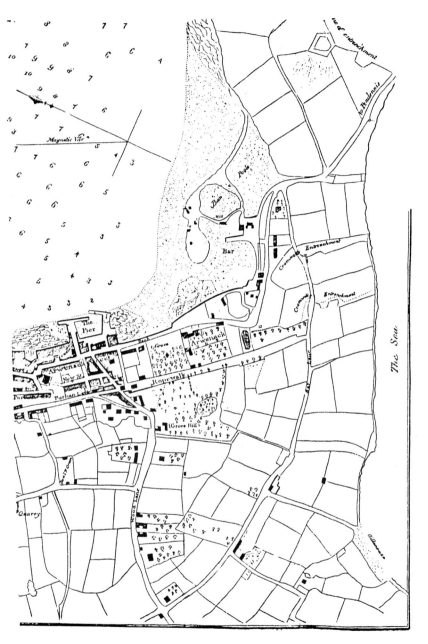

Map: 'History & Description of Town &
Harbour, Falmouth', 1827, showing tide-mill

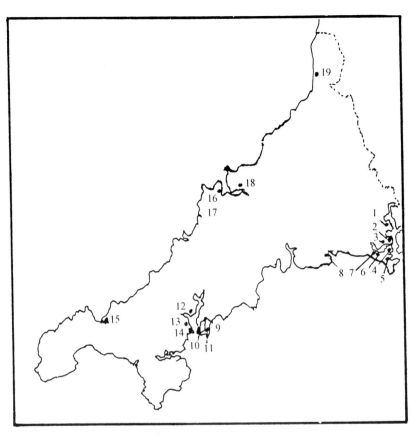

Map of Cornish tide-mills

1   Higher Salter Mills
2   Salter Mill
3   Antony Passage Mill
4   Carbeal Mill
5   Millbrook or Inswork Mill
6   Delabole Mill
7   Wacker Mill
8   Polvellan or Pool Mill
9   Sea Mill, Gerrans
10 Place Mill
11 Froe Mill
12 Penpoll Mill
13 Mylor Bridge Mill
14 Old Bar Mill
15 Hayle Mill
16 Sea Mill, Padstow
17 Trevorrick or St Issey Mill
18 Dinham Mill, St Minver
19 Bude Mill

The tidal rise and fall on the Duchy coast was applied to yet another source of power, the tide-mill. Nineteen have been traced in the county, dating from the fifteenth century on, with seventeen still working in the nineteenth century, and five surviving into the twentieth. Part of a creek, or a suitable shoreline, was pounded off to form a reservoir and an undershot wheel set in a gated sluice to the sea, beside a mill house. The flow of the rising or falling tide to or from the pond set the wheel in motion. Some of these mills must have failed because of the difficulty of finding men willing to work the variable hours set by the tides, as seems to have been the case at Hayle.

CHAPTER 4

The Fisheries

In books lies the soul of the whole Past Time; the articulate audible
voice of the Past, when the body and material substance of it has
altogether vanished like a dream.

Thomas Carlyle

'IT is by the mines and fisheries . . . that Cornwall is compen-
sated for a soil, too barren in many parts of the County, to be
ever well cultivated . . .' said Wilkie Collins in 1851. Though
William Marshall said of East Cornwall that 'the country,
whether in point of soil or cultivation, is above mediocrity'
farming in the west was too often nearer subsistence level. The
farmer's time might have to be divided between his fields and
the mines or the sea. Similarly when weather or catches made it
expedient some fishermen would turn to work on the land or
about the mines. But, with corn dear and sometimes scarce, the
survival of a large proportion of labouring families did depend
on the produce of the sea, particularly on the pilchards.

The pilchard, *Clupea pilchardus* formerly, now *sardina pilchardus*,
which was being caught as early as 1271 at St Goran, has played
a highly important part in the life of the county up to the late
nineteenth century. When shoals of these adult sardines were
small or absent there could be great distress. No observant
traveller or guide-book writer has failed to give long and dramatic descriptions of this peculiarly Cornish industry. The fish is
somewhat smaller than a herring with larger, looser scales, and
readily distinguished by holding it by the dorsal fin when it

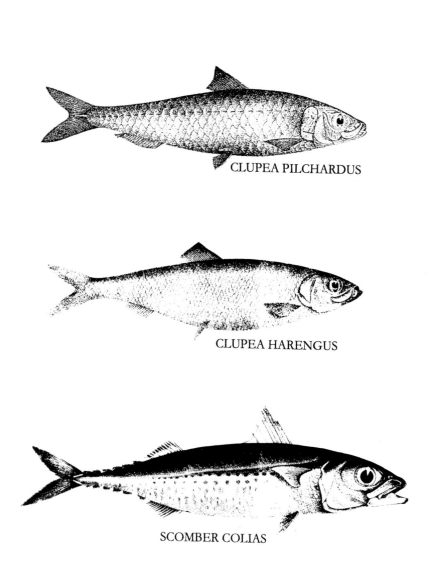

CLUPEA PILCHARDUS

CLUPEA HARENGUS

SCOMBER COLIAS

Pilchard, Herring and Mackerel

hangs horizontally while the herring dips head down. Where they came from and where they went is not certain, but they appeared in July off the Isles of Scilly where the drift-net boats took some. Then they arrived on the mainland coast for the vital inshore fishery in immense quantities in some years, but in others so few as to be useless. They were taken sometimes as far east as Devon, but mainly west of Fowey and Newquay.

There were minor variations in the method of fishing from the various ports and coves, but there was a great measure of common technique. In St Ives alone the fishing was tightly controlled by an Act of Parliament (16 Geo. IV, replaced by 4 Vict. 1841). In July, when the pilchards were expected, a convenient high place above the boat beach was manned by a 'huer' on whose experience and skill the catches would depend. His work was to watch for the tell-tale purplish cloud-like shadow on the sea made by an approaching shoal, to alert the waiting boats with a cry of 'Hevva, hevva,' and then direct them with calls, speaking trumpet or signalling 'bushes' (literally of gorse in bloom, or canvas framed into a one-foot diameter ball) to a successful haul.

The boats used were a seine boat of twelve to fifteen tons burden with a crew of five rowers and a steersman and two to handle the huge net, a similar tow boat or 'follyer' carrying a second smaller stop-net, and a 'lurker' to assist where needed. Guided by the huer the seine boat moved ahead of the shoal and at the signal paid out the seine net while rowing fast to ring round the whole mass of fish. Any gap between the net ends was closed by the stop net. Seine nets were from 190 (347.5 metres) to 300 (548.7 m.) fathoms in length and from 9 (16.5m) to 16 (29.3 m) fathoms in breadth of a fine cod or Dungarvon mesh, corked at the head and leaded at the foot so that they lay on the bottom at their particular station. According to locality they were anchored with grapnels where they lay, or warped into shallow water by 'blowsers', the onshore workers, as a reservoir of fish to be emptied over perhaps a week. In St Ives the seine warp ropes had to be secured ashore before the seine was shot (4 Vict. 16) and at Porthminster wrought iron spindles for capstans (which were taken away out of season) stood until recently.

At St Ives, too, a special disposition of six working areas, called 'stems', was enforced by law, in each of which the various seine companies took turn in the order of their registration. This was necessary as, at the peak of the trade, there were 249 seines in the town, not all necessarily available at any one time. Each company held the stem from midnight to midnight, with variations for each stem governed by the state of the tide, except if their net was shot, when the next in turn could take station.

The next stage, which fascinated many observers, was the process of 'tucking'. With the water being beaten to drive the fish away from the side, the tuck-boat circled inside the seine to drop its net and tie it to the top warp to make a second ring wall. Then, with the seine ringed with boats the tuck-net was raised bringing a seething, sparkling mass of fish to the surface to be scooped up in baskets and poured into the waiting craft. Filled to the gunwales, almost swamping, the boats were pulled ashore and the fish unloaded with wooden shovels into 'gurries', a four-handled box registered as 30 by 21 by 19 inches deep holding 1,000 to 1,200 fish (actually 11 hundreds of 123 by tradition), or as little as 700 of herring.

As each gurry was filled it was rushed to a salting house, a 'palace' in the east, cellar or bulking house in the west, often followed by small boys hoping for the chance of a snatched fish. The fish cellar was an open-centred quadrangle with one- or two-storeyed lean-to shelters against two or three walls, channels in the floor and a collecting point for fish oil, and a salt store.

In the open centre women and girls laid a thin bed of coarse brownish 'bay', imported French sea salt, about four feet wide

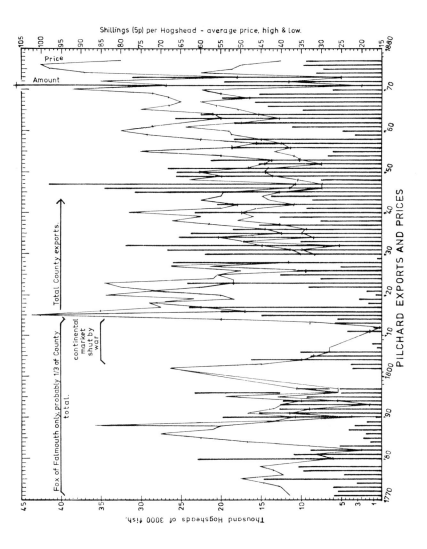

Shillings (5p) per Hogshead – average price, high & low.

Price

Amount

Total County exports.

Fox of Falmouth only, probably 1/3 of County total.

continental market shut by war

Thousand Hogsheads of 3000 fish.

PILCHARD EXPORTS AND PRICES

and as long as was needed. On it were put the pilchards, edgewise and close, and each layer smoothed over with more salt, fish and salt supplied by an endless line of children rushing with buckets as called for, until the bulk stood four feet or more high, a mass of brownish salt broken only by an occasional nose or tail. The fish stayed in bulk for at least thirty-three, usually forty, days while blood, oil and water drained out, not to waste but collected and sold to curriers at 1s.4d. (6½p) a gallon. When the time had passed the fish were broken out of bulk and washed in salt water, and the oil left floating in the wash troughs was skimmed off as 'garbage' to be sold to the soap-boilers.

Once smoked as 'fumadoes' ('fairmaids') or pickled for the export trade, salting was a practice established since the sixteenth

Tucking pilchards, Carbis Bay, 1900

century and followed by the last part of the processing. All round the bulking house, under the lean-to, were holes in the wall for pressing poles, or the walls were built with an overhang, and in the floor a gutter leading to an oil pit. Over the gutter and packed tight the whole way round stood hogsheads, a straight-sided barrel loosely coopered so that they would leak. The pilchards were packed in radially, a lid placed on with a block above, and the pressing pole weighted with a boulder of about 25 lb (11.4 kg) fitted with a hook. When the fish settled the hogshead was topped up, and then once more. After the three pressings the contents were reckoned as 3,000 fish, (though if unusually fat, could be as few as 2,500, but the weight would remain about 476 lb (216 kg). The oil from these pressings varied between 4 and 10 gallons (18 and 45.5 litres) per hogshead and was sold as 'train' for outdoor lamps or paint making. The sale of oil alone was reckoned to pay for the whole cost of the crews, blowsers and women, and the sale of fish therefore almost clear profit for a capital outlay on boats, seines and cellars of £1,000 to £1,200 for each company. When the trade began to decline towards the end of the century bulking was replaced by pickling in brine, the big tanks sometimes being built inside the old cellars.

There was a government bounty of 8s. 6d. (42½p) on every hogshead (phased out by 1819), and the value to the county can be seen from the export figures (illustration 18), apart from the local consumption on which the poor labourer depended so heavily for his family survival. His stock was salted down in 'buzzas', big earthenware pots made in the local potteries. About one third of the export from Fowey, Falmouth, Penzance and St Ives went to Naples, and in order of importance the rest to Venice, Leghorn, Ancona, Genoa, Trieste, Civitavecchia and Malta.

The initial outlay was necessarily a capitalist venture and

unlike the share basis of mackerel and herring boats the crews, huer, blowers and women were employed on a wage for the season by the various companies. Payment varied from port to port, and two examples will serve: at Mevagissey it was 8s. (40p) a week for each man plus one quarter of salt fish or one third of the fresh fish shared; the master seiner had more. At St Ives where a seine crew comprised a huer at £3 a month plus one fiftieth of the owner's fish; a master seiner at 45s. (£2.25) a month plus a guinea (£1.05) for the season; seine men 45s. (£2.25) a month and boys 37s.6d. (£1.87½) a month, plus one tenth of fresh fish between the whole crew. Blowers were paid one eighth of fresh fish or 2s.10d. (14p) a hogshead with no wages. Women in the bulking house got 3d. (1p) an hour with a glass of brandy and bread and cheese every six hours. Children earned much less. The difference between fresh and salt fish allowed was due to the high cost of salt, which carried a tax in the early part of the nineteenth century. It took about a bushel of salt to cure 1,000 fish, and the price of salt was an important factor in the trade and the home.

The final profit came from the 'caff-fish' too damaged for use and sold at 10d. (4p) a bushel for manure, and the old blood-stained oily salt, scales and broken fish which also went to the farms. In 1827 the capital invested in the pilchard fishery was estimated at £441,215, but was down to £279,000 in 1832, with 254 seines in the county, 146 of which were in St Ives, though it is not likely that all would have been serviceable in any one season. Investment returns to the companies were erratic, and probably did not exceed a 10% average on the initial outlay.

The second most important fishery was for mackerel with drift nets. In 1838 123 boats, half from Newlyn, were engaged in the trade, and 240,000 fish were sold to Bristol for £2,000, with also large sales for bait to the Newfoundland cod fishery. Unlike the pilchard fishery few statistics are available.

The herring fishery certainly went back to 1602, said Courtney, but he added that it could not be said that there was a herring fishery in the true sense of it being Cornish. Late in the century this statement would have had to be modified. They were a smaller fish than on the east coast, fished for by drift net, like the mackerel. In 1814 16,000 barrels were taken at St Ives and sold for curing at 12s. (60p) a gurry, but that was an unusual event. In 1816 a St Ives man called Noall started fishing for herring in St George's Channel and the Irish coast, many more following, and by 1836 and 1837 the boats were bringing home £10,000 each season after paying off all their expenses while away. Their main market at that time was Liverpool.

Courtney's summary in 1838 of the Cornish fisherman's year

St Ives herring fleet, 1890

ran: 'February to May, mackerel drifting; May to August, the Irish herring fishery; August and part of September, pilchard seining; September to December, pilchard and mackerel drifting; the remainder of the year preparing for the spring fishery.' This, of course, was a generalisation, and certainly by the end of the nineteenth century there was an inshore herring fishery in November and December for which there were smoke-houses in several ports. Quantities were large enough for special delicacies, such as soft roes, to be separately barrelled for the English markets.

Fish, particularly pilchard and herring, were a vital staple of the local diet, and buzzas were part of most households for the salting of store fish. Buzzas were the product of the Truro potteries, among others, salt-glazed inside and lidded.

The inland villages and farm places were supplied by fishermen's wives, called 'jousters'. Hamilton Jenkin describes 'the Newlyn fishwives ... in their scarlet cloaks and large black beaver hats with the fish itself carried in cowals or specially-shaped baskets, which were supported on the women's backs by a broad band which passed round their hats'.

The *West Briton* of December 26th, 1834 records the death in St Ives of Nancy Humphries aged 54 who 'was noted for many years as supplying the parishes surrounding that place with fish, and has been known to travel more than 20 miles (32 km) a day, carrying upwards of one hundredweight (112 lb or 50.8 kg) of fish on her head.' Another such jouster is on record for carrying her load weekly for many years from Newlyn to Camborne. Hard work indeed with pilchards at 8 or 10 for a penny.

Another home chore, often out of doors for better light, for the fishermen's wives was the knitting of 'guernseys', and the sewing-up of calico for oilskins, then soaked in linseed oil for their men's wear at sea. The knitting, in some hands, became a craft skill of a high order.

In West Cornwall fishing was banned from Saturday night to Sunday night for many years for both religious and market reasons. When, in 1896, Lowestoft boats ignored the ban, hostility in Newlyn burst into riot violent enough to bring a battalion of soldiers and three naval ships to contain it, with no firm settlement from Courts or Parliament. The Sunday rest continued in many ports, notably in St Ives, well into the mid-twentieth century.

Jousters at Newlyn

Ports and Harbours

CORNWALL has only four natural deep-water harbours, the St Germans creek over-shadowed by Plymouth, and the Fowey, Fal and Helford estuaries, but it must be remembered that before the coming of the steamship deep water was not very necessary. The word 'porth' does not mean beach except in the sense of a place where a boat may be safely landed, and in that sense the county was provided with almost innumerable ports round the whole 600 miles of coast. A twelfth to fourteenth century graffito found in the excavated building remains at Tintagel Head showed a very early square-rigged ship which may have been drawn by a watcher as it lay in Tintagel Cove, not a berth many such ships would risk today. Some of the ports in their commercial heyday, like Trevaunance by St Agnes, Port William for Delabole, Hartland Quay and even Portreath, make the mind boggle at the shipmasters' intrepidity to gain what, even by nineteenth century standards, was slight profit at great danger. And danger there certainly was; in the Great October Gale of 1823 seven ships were lost on the beaches of St Ives Bay, and eleven more between there and Land's End. Every gale had its tally of lost men and ships, sometimes appalling as just mentioned, or the Great Blizzard week of March 1891 when twenty-two vessels, including three steamers and a four-masted ship, were lost on Cornish shores alone. Lloyds' estimate in the 1830s was of fifty vessels lost, stranded or dismasted annually, rounding Land's End.

Improvements at the landing places started at a very early date. Looe quay dates from at least as early as 1243, Fowey from even earlier, Polperro's first pier from the fourteenth century and Newlyn's old pier from the fifteenth century. Truro, Penryn, Mousehole, Padstow, Port Isaac, Port Gaverne and Port Quin wharves were all medieval. Boscastle pier dates from about 1547,

Trevaunance Harbour, St Agnes, with schooner *Ystwyth* of Padstow
unloading coal, before 1808 when the boat was wrecked.

and Gweek also dates from the Tudor period or earlier, to increase in importance when mining flourished in the Wendron-Helston area. Whether fishing or trade gave the impetus to set the port building under way needs individual study of each place, and often proves to come from the drive of a single entrepreneur or small group of businessmen. Mousehole and Newlyn were of much greater importance than Penzance in the Middle Ages, but it was merchants who provided the shelter of Penzance's first pier some time before 1512, and again helped to finance the rebuildings of 1745 and 1764-7 which took the town to predominance. The pier was extended in 1813, a new north pier added in 1848, and both north and south piers further lengthened with the lighthouse on the south pier in 1855. The first dry dock in the West Country was built by John Mathews in 1812, realigned and enlarged by N. Holman in 1880. The harbour was further improved with a floating dock opened in 1884, with the swing Ross Bridge of 1881 completing road access to the docks area. Fishing fleets still thronged Newlyn and Mousehole through the nineteenth century but when the new pier greatly enlarged Newlyn in the nineteenth century the fishing trade of local and up-country boats became centred there.

It was the initiative of Sir John Killigrew in the early seventeenth century (plus the security given by St Mawes and Pendennis castles) that raised 'Smithick' from a small collection of fishermen's cottages to a township, and Sir Peter Killigrew after the Civil War who obtained the charter for Falmouth in 1661 and the building of the Town Quay in 1674. By 1688 Falmouth was described by Defoe as 'much the richest and best trading town in this county'. The Packet Service, started in November 1689, maintained Falmouth's lead through the 18th century, and when the new Customs House was built in 1790 the town was noted as having 'many very opulent merchants'. At that time almost one third of the pilchard export trade was through the town. The mining and export trade was steadily lost to other ports in the nineteenth century, leaving very little when the Packet Service ended in 1852, but a new wealth came when the Falmouth Docks Company built the Eastern Breakwater and a dock in 1860-61, and added a second in 1865, the year in which the railway reached the town, further enhancing the importance of the harbour. Falmouth's first dry dock was made at Little Falmouth in 1820.

St Ives' small and inadequate pier (standing about the middle of the north side of the present harbour) was replaced by John Smeaton's fine stone pier in 1770, with a sea-wall to back Porthmeor beach against northerly storms. The pier was extended in 1889 by Sir Edward Hain after the failure of Sir Christopher Hawkins' incomplete northern breakwater, and a west pier added in 1894. Stone ballast to fill the extension was quarried out of Carn Crouse at Porthgwidden, carried by tramway on a wooden viaduct to the site. The broad gauge rails still showing on the quay were for a crane to hoist the timber baulks controlling the sand-flushing arches. The West Pier was used for stone exported by other local quarries.

An Act of 1775 improved Mevagissey, and a large outer harbour was built in 1889-90 costing £22,000, only to be destroyed by the Great Blizzard of 1891. It was rebuilt in 1897 at a further cost of £32,000. In both towns the fisheries must have been the prime consideration, remarkable investments from such small communities. Trevaunance Quay, St Agnes, authorised in 1793 and completed in 1794 at a cost of £10,000, on the other hand, created shelter on an iron-bound coast in an almost impossible place, entirely for the service of the mines, and flourished only while they were thriving locally. It was destroyed by a winter storm in 1916, with a scatter of cut stone its only trace.

On the south coast in the 1790s Charles Rashleigh at West Polmeor carved the Charlestown wet dock and harbour out of solid rock (and kept up its level with water leated all the way from Luxulyan) especially for the china-clay trade. At Pentewan a few miles south, where ships had been beached to load clay, Sir Christopher Hawkins built a very short canal through the beach to a basin in the valley mouth in 1826 for the same trade. A narrow-gauge railway served the port and by 1831, though tiny, it was handling one third of the county's clay exports, soon reduced by frequent sand-choking of the canal. In 1828 the great entrepreneur Joseph Austen (later Treffry) took over the mud-flats of Par to create a new harbour for the china-clay trade and several other industries. A rail and leat viaduct, the first in Cornwall, later joined the clay pits to his port and as a further outlet he extended his horse-drawn railway north to the new harbour built by Richard Lomax at Newquay in 1836.

The booming mining industry needed more and more port facilities in the eighteenth and nineteenth centuries, and local enterprise provided them. The sandy inlet of Portreath on the north coast had a slipway and possibly some shelter on the west side built early in the eighteenth century, and in 1713 there was a proposal to build a pier, but its erection seems uncertain. A pier was finally constructed on the east side in 1760, with the landowner and mine adventurer Francis Basset a moving spirit and investor. By 1771 the coal requirements for one month for Dolcoath mine alone were met by twenty-two ships using the difficult harbour, and Lord de Dunstanville, Francis Basset's son, acquired complete control and repaired and extended the pier between 1778 and 1781. It was then leased by the Foxes of Falmouth and Williamses of Scorrier to serve their large mining interests. At considerable cost an additional basin was excavated to take twenty-five vessels, and the approach roads improved to take the ever-increasing traffic of mules carrying coal and ore. So heavy did that traffic become that a canal was proposed to the Poldice and North Downs mines, but a horse-drawn plateway,

Pentewan Harbour, 1914

the county's first, was built in 1809 instead and continued working until 1866. The final improvements to the harbour were an
extension of the pier in 1824, and a second basin in 1846, with a
bar of timber baulks across the entrance to the basins added later
for the protection of the anchored ships. With all the improvements the port could only be used in reasonably good
weather, as it was up to the 1960s.

Hayle, impaired since the Middle Ages by a sand bar, was also
improved in the eighteenth century for the Cornish Copper
Company by a wharf at Carnsew and a canal cut on the south
side of Phillack Creek to Copperhouse in 1769, as described on
p. 111. John Harvey acquired land at Carnsew in 1779 for a
foundry and shortly after deepened the shallow Penpol Creek. In
1818 his son Henry further deepened the creek and built a great
wharf so that sizeable ships could berth close to the foundry. A
regular packet steamer service to Bristol was added in 1831. As
the firm developed its foundry and mines supplies business a
dry-dock and launching slips were added, and a large pound for
water to flush the sea channel. As at Portreath, a canal was
proposed from Hayle by Angarrack for seven miles to
Carwynnen Bridge to carry the increasing ore exports from the
mines of Camborne and Praze. A railway combining stationary
and locomotive steam power and horses was built in 1837
instead, running to Redruth and extended to Portreath and
Tresavean Mine in 1838. As with so many other Cornish ports
Hayle's fortunes declined as the mines failed in the face of cheap
foreign imports, and the demand for Cornish pumping engines
came to an end.

Porthleven on the south coast was a hamlet in 1800 on a
marshy inlet used only by a few fishermen. In 1811 a Harbour
Company was formed, and with Government money excavated a
basin and started a granite harbour which was completed in 1825
under the supervision of Thomas Telford. One reason for the

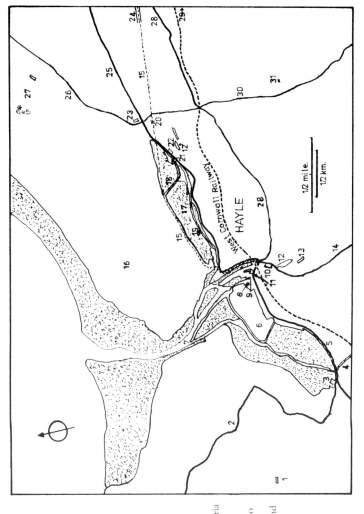

1 Trevethoe, Praed family home
2 St Ives road
3 Grigg's Quay
4 Hayle River
5 The Causeway
6 Harvey's harbour flushing reservoir
7 Long mole, faced with copper-smelting scoria
8 Lime kiln
9 Dry dock
10 Harvey's Foundry
11 Drawing Office and warehouses on Harvey's Quay
12 Mill header ponds
13 Mellanear smelter and hammer mills
14 Helston road
15 Hayle–Redruth railway, 1837
16 Dunes
17 Angarrack Creek
18 Black Road bridge, built of CCC scoria
19 Hayle canal, 1769
20 One of the first railway bridges?
21 Tide mill, destroyed; tailrace runs into canal dock
22 Cornish Copper Company, smelter and foundry
23 Loggans Mill
24 Inclined plane
25 Camborne toll-road
26 Gwithian road
27 Dynamite works
28 Old coaching road
29 Angarrack smelter
30 Fraddam road
31 Wheal Alfred

Plan of Hayle Harbour

building was to create a harbour of refuge, but the reopening of at least ten mines in the neighbourhood after 1810 must also have encouraged the Company. However, the mine owners turned elsewhere and up to 1832 the port was a failure, but from then up to 1846 a steady trade of coal in and copper ore out, for the great Wheal Vor particularly, kept the harbour busy. After this there was a rapid decline as copper and silver-lead production fell off due to awkward lodes, inefficiency and the competition of the East Cornwall mines. Some china-stone and china clay was exported, and when Harvey and Company took control in 1855 building materials, coal and fertilizer imports kept the port alive into the twentieth century.

The mines of Gwennap moved their ores by mule in the early nineteenth century to the nearest inlet, Restronguet Creek on the Fal, where wharves at Point gave a loading site much nearer than Penryn or Falmouth. When John Taylor and Company of London took control of the mines in 1819 their prosperity rapidly developed, and quays, basins and warehouses were built along the creek side at Devoran, served by a horse-drawn railway from 1826. After 1854 the railway was run by steam locomotives up to the First World War. More than half a mile of quays, basins and wharves were fed by a network of sidings, and the line continued on to the quay at Point and its tin smelter. Devoran at its peak in 1835 imported the whole of the 15,000 tons of coal used by the United and Consolidated mines at Gwennap, and at that time was the leading mining port, greater than Portreath or Hayle. Only after the railway was built did Hayle overtake Devoran in importance. Lime-kilns, timber and shipbuilding yards, ship chandlers and inns made the new village a bustling trading complex. Though the output of the copper mines was falling off towards the 1850s a considerable trade in 'mundic' (iron pyrites or arsenopyrites) kept the port busy, and an extension to Wheal Buller also helped, with tin ingots from

Carnkie. After the seventies the port steadily declined, the trade becoming mainly the import of coal, and the creek is now silted up with the waste from the mines which it once served.

The largest inlet on the north coast is the estuary of the Camel, a harbour of some importance in prehistoric and later times with trade across the Bristol Channel and to Ireland. The entrance channel, though, is narrow and dangerous with shifting sandbanks and the dangerous Doom Bar. In the eighteenth century ore from nearby mines was exported, and coal, timber and salt imported. Only as late as 1830 was an effort made to provide safety measures, a daymark on Stepper Point and capstans to warp ships into the river, and later buoys, lights and pilotage controlled by Harbour Commissioners. Padstow became a prosperous port in the nineteenth century with ship-building and general trade, and a regular steam-packet service to Hayle and Bristol. Later, ships used the port for the increasing flow of emigrants to America. The port continued busy into the twentieth century. Wadebridge, further upstream, which could only be reached by sea-going ships on a high spring tide, developed in the nineteenth century for the export of granite from the De Lank quarries, and some china clay and iron ore, but its activity did not last for very long.

Bude also offered tidal harbourage and a wet basin, but its trade was basically agricultural (see p. 112).

Mining, while creating a need for ports, also destroyed some of the older ports and wharfages by greatly increasing the silt washed down into the creeks; for instance the one-time port of Tregony now has nearly four kilometres of water meadows beside a narrow Fal where once shipping sailed. The Helford and Camel rivers have abandoned quays, and opposite the granite quays of Penryn two feet of mud cover a bed of 4 and 5-inch wide oyster shells.

Boat Building

WITH the exception of ports like Trevaunance, Tintagel or Port William where loading of cargoes was by sheer-legs from above, and whose existence was solely tied to local mineral workings, shipbuilding was almost universal. As long as ships were small and timber built all the larger ports had shipwrights and ship-yards, some with a county-wide reputation for their quality, like Padstow, Newquay, St Ives and Porthleven. Smaller boats were often built on the open beach, with each district having its characteristic popular lines, particularly in the eighteenth and early nineteenth centuries. The boats of West Cornwall had a strong similarity to those of Brittany, and were always clinker built with pointed sterns west of the Lizard. Even some of the smallest coves had a reputation for good design, like the crab-bers of Porthgwarra.

The three main types of fishing boat built were the seine boats already mentioned, three-masted luggers and two-masted mackerel driving luggers. The first of those sailing boats was about thirty-five feet in length and twelve to fifteen feet beam, and often sailed as far as Ireland or Scotland after herring. The mackerel drifters were about fifty feet long with a fourteen foot beam, and packed the harbours until late in the nineteenth century and after.

Shipwrights' wages in the 1830s were 15s. (75p) a week, and had only risen to 21s. (£1.05) in the 1880s, with apprentices starting at 2s. (10p) a week rising by 1s. a week for seven years, and a foreman 24s. (£1.20) at the later date. Their working day was from 6 a.m. to 6 p.m., except in winter when it was from dawn to dusk.

The first iron-hulled steamer to be built in the county was a paddle tug for Germany from Harveys of Hayle in 1846, and a steady line of ships followed from that yard until late in the century, including a steamer of 3,800 tons and the county's first steam lugger, the *Patmos* of St Ives, in the 1870s.

One remarkable shipping venture was the Hain Line of St Ives. Edward Hain, son of a shipmaster, bought the 100 ton *Camilla* in 1832, sailing her himself, and building up a small sailing fleet. His son, also Edward, followed him, trading coastwise and throughout the Mediterranean. By 1876 the line registered six ships, all built out of the county, with an iron barquentine of 276 tons built in Hayle added in 1877. In 1878 the iron steamship SS *Trewidden* of 1,800 tons, built in South Shields, was bought, the first of 35 steamers in the nineteenth century. 105 more were built in the twentieth until the line was incorporated into the P & O fleet in the mid-century.

The dry dock in Penzance, probably the first in the county, was open in 1814, cut out of the rock by a Mr Matthews, and rebuilt for Holman and Sons when the wet-basin and Ross Bridge were built in 1884. There was a dry dock at Little Falmouth as early as 1820 built by a Mr Symons, followed by the docks of the Falmouth Dock Company at Pendennis after 1858, and in 1868 the Docks Foundry and Engineering Company floated by the ships' chandler Cox Brothers, which, as Green, Silley and Weir, carried the ship servicing industry well into the twentieth century. Harvey's of Hayle built a dry dock for their ships about 1834, which, long disused, was filled in about 1964.

Much of the timber for shipbuilding and wharves was imported, some from Norway, the Americas or elsewhere. Some was 'seasoned' by lying in water, often for years; timber for Falmouth Docks lay in rafts contained by chained floating baulks in Penryn creek, and also in a pond at the lower end of the Foxes Grovehill estate where the railway crosses Avenue Road. Seasoning ponds are not easily traceable, or, like the Penryn rafts, leave no mark at all. The photograph on p. 61 is a fine example.

In the 1830s when British foreign trade was increasing Scillonian ship-building received a great boost, and with the better education established by Augustus Smith in 1850 (see p. 151) islanders were well-placed to officer the growing fleet, while their fellows on the mainland could only serve before the mast.

Smuggling

WITH taxation imposed from a distant London, unknown to most Cornish and virtually a foreign place, and with Roscoff and other French ports easily reached, it is hardly surprising that it was acceptable to many to make their own rules. The Cornishman's desire to lose as little profit as possible after the difficulties and dangers of winning tin established a smuggling trade in Elizabethan times and later, but the increasing taxes to support the wars of the seventeenth and eighteenth centuries widened the scope of the 'free trade' to luxury goods, brandy, gin, rum, tobacco, tea, salt, silk, lace, china and glass. Up to the 1840s smuggling was a widespread and almost respectable trade, reaching a peak when the forces of law were diverted to meet the needs of the war with France from 1798 to 1815. At almost every port, cove and beach between Hartland Point and Cawsand cargoes were landed at some time. The busiest part of Cornwall for contraband was the coast between Polperro and Plymouth Sound, and it was at Polperro that the first Preventive boat was stationed in 1801. Falmouth, where the Packet Service crews used their special advantages, the Lizard coves, Mount's Bay and St Ives Bay had a very active trade. Even the less easily reached north coast was regularly used wherever a cove, however difficult to reach, offered the prospect of an unobserved landing.

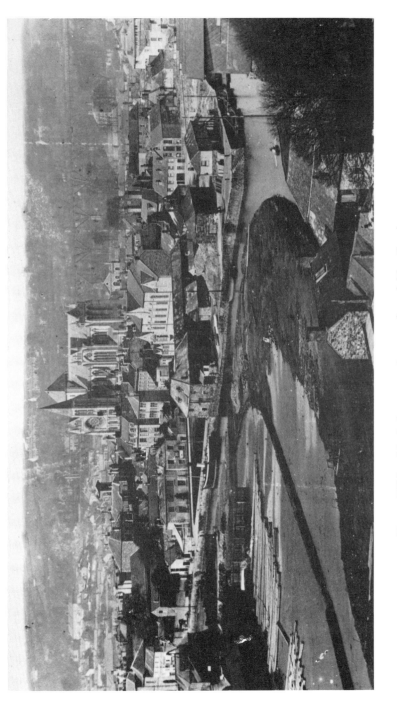

Truro, 1896, with timber seasoning ponds and *New Resolve* steamer.

Despite the vigilance of Revenue men and Preventive boats, assisted only too often in the corrupt eighteenth century by the connivance of the gentry and the laxity of Customs Officers' morality, an observer of 1800 (quoted in the Victoria County History *Maritime History of Devonshire*) could surmise that more brandy and rum was run in Dorset, Devon and Cornwall than was imported into London legally. He believed that some 40,000 men were involved in smuggling, and it must be assumed that a large part of those must have come from Devon and Cornwall. Polwhele suggested that in 1805 some 337,200 gallons of wine and spirit and 110 tons of tobacco and salt were run. The small coin shortage of the late eighteenth century has been attributed to be in part due to the amount being sent abroad, local token coins being minted to ease trade.

Three main methods were used to bring the goods in. First was the run ashore in a convenient obscure cove under cover of night, when local knowledge was essential, and the goods then moved inland on horse and mule to secure hiding places. Second was the sinking of strings of tubs offshore to await the right moment for collection, and third the exchange of goods at sea between fishing boats, to be landed with the catch. Whoever made the main profit, the men who moved the goods ashore earned 1s. (5p) with a 5s. (25p) bonus for a successful run.

Small cutters or fishing boats were the usual vessels for the trade in Cornwall, rarely armed, though the men themselves on many occasions used violence to keep or recover the cargoes they had run. The battle, both of wits and physical force, between free traders and Preventive men is a fascinating part of the County's past, and no small contributor to the store of legend.

Best known among the smugglers was John 'King of Prussia' Carter (1770-?1807) of Breage, near Helston, and his brother Henry (died 1829). They were never caught smuggling, and even armed their hideaway Bessy's (Prussia) Cove with cannon until John disappeared in 1807.

In the eighteenth century smuggling made the difference between destitution and survival for the hard-pressed Scillonians, and flourished until the Napoleonic War and a new vigilant Preventive Service made it unprofitable.

CHAPTER 5

Mining and Miners

The Cornish miner is simply the most ill-paid, patient, hard-working mortal on the face of the earth'

Tin, 1888, Edward Bosanketh

'THE West of England mining district has yielded metallic minerals to the value of upwards of 200 million sterling [say 1.7 billion today]. In getting this, hundreds of miles of shafts have been sunk and thousands of miles of galleries driven. Forests of timber have been used to support the ground, while mountains of ore and rivers of water have been brought to the surface with the aid of fleets laden with coal,' was J.H. Collins summary in 1897.

The winning of tin and copper goes back at least into the Bronze Age; for instance, an early copper ingot at Gillan, Meneage; Bronze Age pottery remains of *c*. 1,000 BC under the late Iron Age round of Trevisker in St Mawgan which held a hoard of stream tin; and a late Bronze Age site at Kynance, among others, showed tin or copper smelting traces. Little seems known of early copper mining, but prehistoric winning of heavy cassiterite grains from stream beds and often from deep under a barren overburden of sediment, is well attested, as at Carnon Creek, Devoran. Bronze was greatly prized in the Iron Age, and again Cornwall must have made its contribution. Many Iron Age sites show remains of tin smelting, for instance small smelting pits in Chun Castle, but not all are readily dateable. There is a marked concentration of such finds in west Cornwall compared with central and east.

Cornish miners underground

Roman interest in Cornish metals was apparently minimal until between AD 250 and AD 340 as implied by the sizeable coin hoards found in the tin-streaming areas. Production was possibly left in native hands, but pewter vessels were common-place in Roman Britain during the same period but not on the Continent, and probably a British invention. Pieces have been found at Bosence in St Erth, Caerhays and Hallivick in St Stephen-in-Brannel. A wedge-shaped tin ingot from Carnanton in St Mawgan-in-Pydar carried a stamp suggesting a fourth century date, but other ingots are less exactly dated.

Finds of small tin pieces have been made in some Dark Age sites, and that the trade continued is suggested by a reference in the *Life of St John the Almsgiver, Patriarch of Alexandria* (died AD 616), to an Alexandrian seaman of his time who sailed to Britain with grain, relieving a famine, and returning with a cargo of tin (Hencken, p.201). The first documentary evidence is an entry in the Pipe Rolls of 1156 noting taxes on tin from Devon and Cornwall. Worth quotes the method of smelting in 1198.

Lodes with copper above and tin below occur mainly in or near the granite bosses of the south-western peninsula, and erosion of the Armorican mountain chain under which they lay has left many at the present surface. Washed out cassiterite – 'stream tin' – sources were limited and as they were worked out were replaced by open 'goffans' on to the lodes, and shallow shafts deepening as pumping was introduced and improved.

A mine was opened where the source lode found during streaming, a cliff exposure, or a line of blackthorn on a moor showing underground water or other clue suggested a possible lode. It was financed by 'Adventurers', people with not neces-sarily much money to risk, who could hold shares in almost any fraction of the capital. In proportion to their share they put up enough cash for the men and tools to sink a shaft and start work on the lode. The hope always was that the ore would be rich

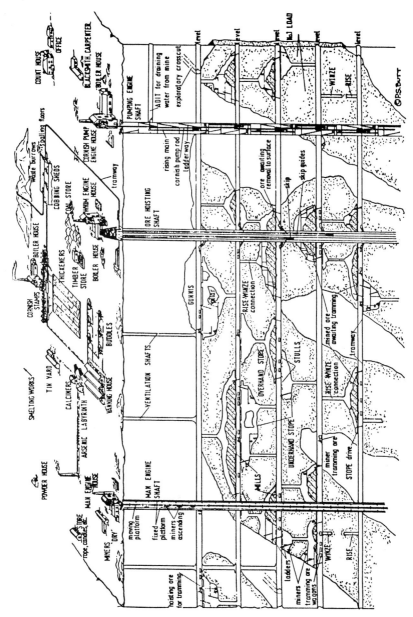

Cornish mine in section

enough immediately to pay for further costs, but if this did not happen further calls in proportion were made until the mine started to pay. At the end of the working year came 'Account Day' when the accounts were balanced, the state of the mine presented by the Captain and the Purser, the ores sampled and a dividend or a call declared to the adventurers in proportion to their shares. This was the Cost Book system, almost universal in Cornwall. It had the major disadvantage that the mine never built up reserves of capital to meet lean times or special new needs such as a Cornish pumping engine. Heavy capital costs or litigation by dissatisfied adventurers might cause the mine to close even when rich, or have to be newly floated by fresh adventurers. Apart from these other costs the mine paid the ground landlord one fifteenth, on average, of the profits, many becoming extremely wealthy without venturing a penny or a minute of time for their fortune.

The mine was managed by 'captains' whose badge of office was a white jacket. The 'Grass Captain' oversaw all surface work, and one or more 'Underground Captains' the working below. The latter were skilled miners, surveyors and geologists on whose skill the success or failure of a mine very much depended. They had to be men of great ability though trained only by experience. It was the captains usually who decided on the drives to be cut, judged the tributers' bids, chose the men, kept the cost sheets and oversaw the ore sampling. For all these duties they took home £6 to £8 a month in the nineteenth century.

The book-keeping, wages and disbursement were managed by the Purser, who was also responsible for dividing the profits. His pay was usually the same as the captains, but only in the larger mines. The four highest paid workers on the mine were the engineman; the binders, who saw to the timbering; the pitman, who looked after the shafts, ladders and raising the ore; and the head smith. They each earned from £2 to £2.60 per month.

Miners earned from 80p to £1.05 a month, and 'landers' who raised the ore about £1.20. The 'grass men' on the tin dressing floors earned about 90p, and 'spallers', the women who broke up the ores by hand, about 52p a month. Children earned very much less, boys going underground at about 14, but not unusually much younger. All these wages apply to the late eighteenth century but the nineteenth century did not see any very substantial improvement. Poor as the wages were, miners were subject to 'spales' or fines for refusing extra duty, or going off wrecking.

Cornish miners were employed in two different ways. Those on a regular wage, however rich or poor the lode might be, were called 'tut-workers' but were usually set to work on drives or adits where no profit was to be made. The hopefully profitable mining was done by 'tributers' who were, in effect, self-employed. They contracted to work a given 'pitch' for a proportion of the value of the ore won, often providing all their own tools, candles and gunpowder. W. Philip wrote in 1815 that 'if the tributer, after covering the cost of tools, and repairing them, together with such candles and powder as he may use, and the charge of drawing his work to surface and rendering it merchantable by the women and children whom he employs, contrives to gain 20 shillings (£1.0) a week for himself, he considers he has made a decent living.'

Work was organised on a monthly basis by a kind of Dutch auction. The under-ground captain with a clerk took a position well above a waiting group of miners, and a pitch, or piece of work, would be named by the captain. A tributer would bid, and perhaps be underbid by another; when bidding ceased the captain tossed a pebble in the air and any further bid had to be made before it touched the ground. The last bid would be the price in the pound of the value of the ore the tributer was prepared to work for. He usually bid on behalf of a 'pare', a

working team of six to eight men. The tributers gambled on
their knowledge of the lodes to make a good profit from a rich
spot, but if their judgement was wrong they could be hard put
to survive the next month. The mine captain, too, was pitting
his knowledge against theirs. Pitches not taken up were offered
at a price, usually taken up by outbid tributers, simply to be
employed even when profit was not expected.

After the setting of the pitches the captains, purser, doctor
and other employees drew their salaries, and the merchants' bills
were paid. The men who bid for their pares then came to draw
their shares to divide among their group. They were followed by
the tut-workers for their wages, with the daymen and labourers.
The 'bal-maidens' (female surface-workers) followed and finally
the children, some under ten years old. Pay day was always a
holiday. However, pay was commonly by the calendar month,
not four-weekly, making a five-week spell before settlement
several times a year. Resentment for the practice led to strikes in
many areas, and in 1872 Tincroft Mine at Illogan turned to the
fairer deal, soon followed by most other mines.

The miners' working clothes were a jacket, shirt and trousers
of coarse drill. They wore low-vamped shoes without socks, and
a bowler hat stiffened with resin on which was a lump of clay
with a candle stuck into it. Hanging from a button on his coat
would be a bundle of up to ten candles to last out his six-hour
'core' or shift (South Crofty made a daily allowance of six). His
tools, carried down and up the shaft every shift were usually a
Cornish shovel, the short miners' pick, one or more 'borryers'
(drills), a sledge hammer and wedges, a 'needle' or long nail,
tamping bar, charger and scraper, and supply of rushes or quills
if blasting was to be done or perhaps safety fuses after the 1830s.
Carrying this 20 to 30 lb load over hundreds of feet of ladders,
before the 'man-engine' was introduced, contributed greatly to
miners' short lives.

MINER'S TOOLS.

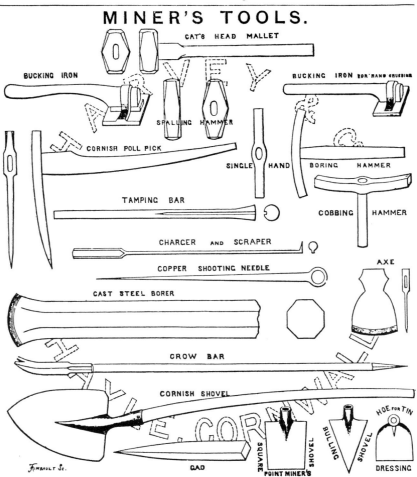

CAT'S HEAD MALLET

BUCKING IRON

BUCKING IRON FOR HAND CRUSHING

SPALLING HAMMER

CORNISH POLL PICK

SINGLE HAND

BORING HAMMER

TAMPING BAR

COBBING HAMMER

CHARGER AND SCRAPER

COPPER SHOOTING NEEDLE

AXE

CAST STEEL BORER

CROW BAR

CORNISH SHOVEL

HOE FOR TIN

SQUARE

BULLING SHOVEL

SHOVEL

DRESSING

GAD

POINT MINER'S

In the above Illustration we have only shown a few of the Miner's Tools as used in Cornwall. There are now so many different kinds in use in the various mining localities, that to give illustrations of all would be a work requiring a catalogue to itself. Mining Engineers therefore would do well if they sent sketches of the Tools they require, or it would give us sufficient information if they stated that they required Tools as used in Cornwall, California, or the Queensland District.

186 & 187, Gresham House, London, E.C.

A page from Harvey's catalogue

WILLIAMS' PERRAN FOUNDRY CO.

THE CORNISH PUMPING ENGINE,

FOR DRAINING MINES, SUPPLYING TOWNS, &c.

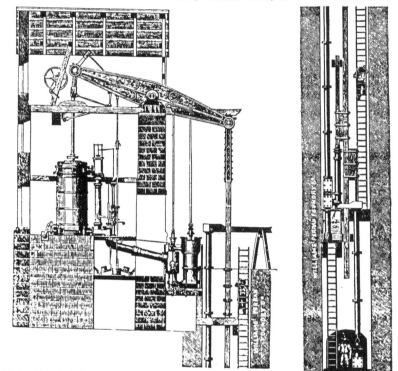

The above illustration clearly shows the usual method of Draining Mines, and notwithstanding all the Improvements in rotatory Engines it is still the most economical method of raising water.

It is of the first importance in Mining operations where it is necessary to employ Machinery for Draining, that the whole should be practically and judiciously laid out.

Very much depends on the constructive proportions of Machinery, and the careful execution of the details to ensure economy, and it is in these essential particulars that Williams' Perran Foundry Co. possess such an immense advantage, both from the magnitude and variety of the works they have completed, and their lengthened experience in mining and pumping.

Williams' Perran Foundry Co. continue to devote the greatest attention to make these Engines worthy of the credit they have received from Engineers and others in all parts of the World, and from their abundant manufacturing facilities, are in a position to supply at the shortest possible notice every description of this class of Machinery, and (by a large stock) in many cases to anticipate the wants of their clients.

The Taylor's Engine at the United Mines, Cornwall, was made by the Williams' Perran Foundry Co., and has performed the highest duty ever registered, having raised 107,000,000 lbs. of water, 1 foot high, per 1 bushel of coal.

Estimates for Engines with Pumps, &c., complete, to suit the various depths and quantities of water to be raised, &c., on application.

PERRANARWORTHAL, CORNWALL,

AND

1 & 2 GREAT WINCHESTER STREET BUILDINGS, LONDON, E.C.

A page from Williams' catalogue

The man-engine, first devised and applied in Germany in the 1830s, was actively promoted by the Royal Cornwall Polytechnic Society and the Fox clan of Falmouth and a design by the engineer Michael Loam was tried at Tresavean Mine in 1842, driven by water-wheel and working successfully for seventeen years. The principle of the machine was to fix 'sollars' or small steps on the mine pump rods at a spacing equal to the pump stroke, with platforms in the shaft to match. Miners ascended or descended travelling on the rod as it moved in the needed direction and waiting on the platforms as it returned. Some were worked by water-wheel, but most by steam power, to great benefit to the miners' health. Accidents were very few in relation to the number of journeys made, and even when the rods broke, as happened in several mines, injuries were remarkably few with no deaths. Only at the last man-engine in use, at Levant Mine in October 1919, did a broken rod bring fatalities. With a full load of 150 men coming off shift the rod broke at surface and smashed through its safety catches. Thirty-one miners died, eleven were seriously injured, and many more suffered lesser hurt. The man-engine was never used again.

Women were never employed underground, unlike in the coal mines, but worked at the surface 'spalling', breaking up and sorting the ores, often helped by boys. They also worked at the 'buddles', slime pits and washing tables (as did older men and boys) too often wet-footed and cold. These were the bal-maidens, customarily in broad-brimmed hat or bonnet, and despite the dirty work priding themselves on a clean white apron every day.

The health of the men and their families was looked after by the 'bal-surgeon' for 2d. (less than 1p) per man per month (see p. 152). One doctor could serve several mines, and give service to the whole parish also, but there was little that the medicine of the great centuries of mining could do to redress the damage from rock-dust, heavy work in hot wet ends, the heavy candle smoke and choking fumes from black gunpowder, and the immense labour of climbing down and up the ladders of ever-deepening shafts. The churchyards and registers of Cornish mining parishes bear silent witness to the terrible toll the search for metals exacted from the Cornish people. Yet the slow decline of mining in the later nineteenth century drove Cornish men, not to different work, but out to every new mining field round the world.

Everywhere a capricious industry, subject to boom and slump, Cornish mining was no exception. Copper mining was of much less importance than tin in the sixteenth and seventeenth centuries, boomed to greater importance than tin between 1740 and 1776 when the number of mines working copper trebled, only to be brought to a near standstill when the Parys Mine in Anglesey flooded the market after 1768. There was a steady recovery from 1800 to complete domination of World output in the 1830s and on to a peak in the 1850s, particularly in the Chacewater-Camborne area and Devon great Consols on the border, with a steady decline as new fields were opened abroad almost to an end by 1900.

Tin production rose, with fluctuations, up to the 1790s, slumped and then rose to a peak in 1870, falling steadily afterwards, outpriced by Australian and Malayan alluvials and lode ore later from Bolivia.

Every downward turn in metal prices, or mine failure, brought great hardship to the miners. Even though it was usual for miners to open a patch of land to cultivate beside the poor stone or cob homes they built for themselves on the moors, invariably with a pig-sty attached, they could lay by few reserves against hard times. As D.B. Barton suggests in *Tin Mining and Smelting in Cornwall*, 'The harsh truth of the Cornish miner's working life is . . . (that) . . . it was a miserable, dangerous, and even squalid, existence ... he was more frequently the rent-owing occupier of a damp cottage, gaunt on a diet of potatoes and pilchards, and addicted to the local beer-shop.' It is not surprising that serious food riots occurred at least fourteen times in the eighteenth century and four in the nineteenth. In 1775, when the price of tin had fallen low, miners rioted through West Cornwall, smashing all Wedgwood's and other Staffordshire ware that was replacing pewter, one of the staple consumers of tin.

CHAPTER 6

Smelting

Then doth each man carry his portion to the blowing-house, where the same is melted with charcoal fire, blown by a great bellows moved with a water-wheel, and so cast into pieces of a long and thick squareness, from three hundred to four hundred pound weight, at which time the owners' mark is set thereupon.

R. Carew

LITTLE remains of the earliest tin 'blowing' or smelting houses, other than descriptions by visitors to the county, but at Goldherring, in Sancreed, a re-used Romano-British site held an early smelter of probable thirteenth century date. The granite 'castle', an oval structure of 3 feet x 2 feet axis and over 2 feet high, was fed from below by an air-duct running through the defence wall of the settlement, both packed with gorse charcoal with traces of stream-tin grains. This may have been 'blown' by a wind-scoop, as the site is high on a hill away from water, like the 'boles' of other regions. Throughout the western region similar simple smelters must have been used in the Middle Ages, as Worth's Dartmoor description given here suggests: 'In the blowing-house a formal furnace was constructed and the fire was urged by a bellows, actuated by a small water-wheel . . . it is not safe to date the earliest blowing-house before 1300, or . . . to place its possible date more than a few years later. For at least four centuries the blowing-house remained the sole device for smelting tin ore . . . Carew, writing in 1602, refers to enlarged

Plan of tin stamping mill, W. Borlase, *Natural History of Cornwall*, 1758

WILLIAMS' PERRAN FOUNDRY CO.

WATER WHEEL DRIVING STAMPS,

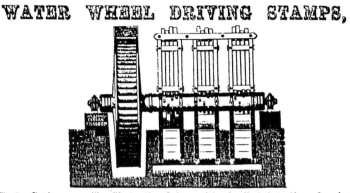

The above Sketch represents a Water Wheel working a Stamps, consisting of 12 Heads, for breaking up Ore and preparing it for dressing, or separating the Mineral from the Rubbish. In some of the large Cornish Mines, Steam Power is used to work a great number of these Heads or Stampers, which are usually constructed with long iron lifters instead of wood. It will be seen from the illustrations that Lifters are fixed in the Barrel, which is caused to revolve by means of a Water Wheel or other motive power; there are also Lifters in the uprights, which are secured to the Stampers; the Heads are thus raised from 9 to 12 in. high, consecutively, and falling their full weight (from 3 to 5 cwt. each) on the Ore, break it in pieces and reduce it to powder.

This illustration shows another arrangement of the Battery, each set consisting of 6 Heads of Stamps.

Though from time to time a great many machines for Crushing and Grinding in different ways have been devised, with a view to supersede the Cornish Stamps, nothing has, however, yet been found which does the work either for Gold, Silver, or Tin, in such a cheap and effectual manner.

PRICES ON APPLICATION.

PERRANARWORTHAL, CORNWALL,
AND

1 & 2 GREAT WINCHESTER STREET BUILDINGS, LONDON, E.C.

A page from Williams' catalogue

and improved "chimneys" for catching the flue dust with its content of tin. But not until the years 1705 or 1706 did the reverberatory furnace threaten its predominance.'

At this early period, and even to the eighteenth century, the richest ore, like that from Pentewan, was smelted direct, but the poorer was first 'crazed' or crushed by pounding in hollows in hard rock, mortar and pestle style. Elvan blocks so used were to be seen in the Cober valley below Helston, and a large surface of granite was hollowed for similar use between three cottages at the top of Zennor Carn, now under a new house, The Carne. By the early seventeenth century crazing was being carried out by a line of iron-shod poles lifted by water-wheel over hard stone basins. Stamps of this form, with elaborations, continued in use to the twentieth century.

Crushed ore was raked against a stream of water in a gulley or wood flume lined with heavily-rooted turf which trapped the heavy cassiterite. Crushing of pebbles, 'shoad stone' – the naturally broken lode near the surface – and the lode, hand-picked and hammered to fist size, was carried out in a flow of water, and all the remaining recovery processes were to separate the cassiterite from lighter waste. The pulp from the stamps was washed into a line of three settling pits. The settlings from the first pit were treated in a square buddle, 7 feet by 3 feet by 2 feet deep, at the head of which was a sloping 'jagging board' with small ridges down the slope. Tin-stuff was spread on the board in a flow of water and slowly washed down stirred by a broom. The larger material was 'tozed'(stirred with a shovel in a wooden 'kieve' or tub), and the poorer material skimmed off, the process repeated if necessary. Later buddles were circular with a sweeping brush turned by water-wheel round the gentle conical slope. The finer material in the second and third pits was run into a circular pit called a 'pednam', stirred up to flow slowly into an 8 ins. deep pit 3 feet wide and 10 feet long divided about one third along by a board. The larger material settling in the first section went to the 'frames', and the second part re-washed.

Frames were two large flat wooden boards, a level head on which ore was spread in ridges, and the body gently sloping. Water evenly distributed at the head washed over the frame as the tin settled and fine waste washed away. At each stage the product was tested with a 'vanning shovel', as in gold panning.

The final 'slimes' were very difficult to treat and wasted tin, and when possible the stamps were adjusted to avoid crushing too fine. Waste was substantial with less than 70% being recovered, and after 1860 this led to a new form of streaming, waste slimes from the mines being worked by various concerns down the valleys right to the sea. Even in the twentieth century recovery from the sea-bed off Gwithian, Hayle, was attempted, almost certainly on ancient as well as recent deposits, and also from old waste tips and some valley bottoms. This labour-intensive and time-consuming method, with producers' individual variations, continued through much of the nineteenth century.

The chief copper ore was chalcocite, locally redruthite, 70% copper, easily powdered, so crushing was only used on very hard ores. The ore was hand-sorted from the waste and the 'prills' of pure ore set aside. Large lumps of mixed ore and low-value stuff such as chalcopyrite were broken down by men, spalled and 'cobbed' – freed of as much waste as possible – by bal-maidens, as was the pure metal 'native copper' from Gwennap and other areas. In the eighteenth century the ore was crushed by girls with 'bucking hammers' on iron plates, but roller crushing replaced hand-work in the nineteenth. The crushed ore was cleaned in the same way as tin ores.

John Harris (1820-1884) in *My Autobiography* in 1882 describes how 'At ten years of age my father took me with him to Dolcoath Mine, to work on the surface, in assisting to dress and

Wheal Friendly, Trevaunance Cove

Tin streaming on beach, Trevaunance Cove, 1920s

prepare copper ore for the market. Sometimes I had to work at the keeve [a hooped barrel where rough ore is washed over a sieve], sometimes at the picking-table, sometimes in the slide [surface delivery point for ore], sometimes on the floors, sometimes in the cobbing-house, and sometimes at the hutch [where the fine ores were sifted in water]. Sometimes I had to wheel the mineral in a barrow until the skin came off my hands, and my arms were deadened with the heavy burden. Sometimes I was scorched with the sun until I almost fainted, and then I was wet with the rains of heaven so that I could scarcely put one foot before another. I left my home at six in the morning, and returned to it again at six in the evening. Yet I never complained . . . After toiling in this way for two years, my father took me with him into the interior of the earth, nearly two hundred fathoms under the surface. Ascending and descending the ladders, some sixty or seventy in number, was a fearful task. On my first descent into the mine, when I was about thirteen years of age, my father went before with a rope fastened to his waist, the other end of which was attached to my trembling self . . . But the climbing up evening after evening, that was the task of tasks! . . .'

Ninety-two years old Mrs Minnie Andrews of Beacon, Camborne, described her work at Wheal Frances, which she started aged about twelve, in the *Cornishman* of April 4th,1967, as follows: 'We walked across the moors to be there for seven o'clock start in the morning. We had twenty minutes crowst time and half an hour for dinner and we worked through till after five o'clock. When Wheal Frances closed and I was eighteen I got a month just one shilling for each year of my age – I got just 18s.(90p) a month and I worked harder than some of the men.' That would have been in 1893.

Deep lode mining inevitably brought unwanted ores with the tin and copper, particularly of iron with sulphur and arsenic.

These were dealt with by the process of 'calcining', at first by roasting the ore in heaps in the open, later in special furnaces with tall chimneys. The ore was fed through a hole over the hearth and fired until the white smoke from the chimney cleared. The white smoke was arsenic oxide which devastated the country round, as for example the Bissoe valley between St Day and Devoran which was a major centre of arsenic production. In the 1870s the fabulously rich Devon Great Consols and other mines in the Callington-Tavistock area, producing about half of the world's copper output, were great arsenic sources also.

In the mid-nineteenth century the Brunton revolving-hearth calciner came into common use and the fumes were passed through the long flues, up to 1,000 feet, of a 'labyrinth' to condense arsenic oxide before finally being discharged from a high stack. All mines with 'foul' ores used calciners with labyrinths, and a good example treating the lead-silver ores of Swanpool Mine, Falmouth, with its stack on Pennance Point, lay partly complete to the 1950s. From the 1880s until after the First World War refined arsenic, used as an insecticide by American cotton farmers, was an important part of mining income.

The simple pit hearth, with stream tin ore thrown on an open fire, mode of smelting is mentioned at the beginning of this chapter, and was later improved by the use of 'Jews' Houses'. These are described by A.K. Hamilton Jenkin in *The Cornish Miner* as 'inverted cones of hard clay, about three feet broad at the top and three feet deep. A blast of air conveyed by a common bellows to the lower part of the furnace served to create an intense heat, and the molten tin discharged from a small opening at the foot.' The term Jews must derive from the fact that many of the buyers came from the Mediterranean and were Jewish traders, not Phoenicians. There must be some connection between this and the legend of Joseph of Arimathea coming to the West Country to buy tin. By the early Middle

Ages the simple blowing house was in use, turf and stone thatched huts with a 'castle' as described on p. 76, where the thatch was periodically burnt off to recover tin blown into the roof.

By the mid-eighteenth century the furnaces were described by Pryce as tall, iron-cramped granite structures with a hearth 6 feet deep, 2 feet square at the top narrowing to 14 inches at the base. The charge of charcoal and black tin in alternate layers was blasted by two bellows working alternately by water-wheel power and the metal cast into blocks of 200 to 300 pounds weight. Hatchett in his tour diary of 1796 describes a similar furnace at St Austell, with an internal form of a double cone, with, from its top, 'a long inclined chimney of about 20 fathoms in length which terminates ... in a circular building which receives the tin accidentally raised by the heat', the failing common to all the blast furnaces. Hatchett also describes copper furnaces at Hayle which were 'Reverberators somewhat resembling those used for tin at St Austle but larger.' He adds that the Hayle furnaces were built of moulded blocks of scoria, and the black blocks can be seen widely round the Hayle area in hedges and buildings today, in the docks and the long embankment between the Penpol and St Erth streams in the harbour.

Copper smelting started at Neath, Glamorgan, South Wales, in 1583, at Bristol and Redbrook on the Wye in the 1680s, and at Swansea in 1717 when the coinage was first made from British copper, all based on ores shipped from Cornwall. Various unsuccessful attempts were made to smelt copper at the mines, for instance at St Ives, Phillack, St Agnes and Pentewan, but it was when the Cornish Copper Co. established a smelter at Carn Entral near Camborne in 1745 that an effective start was made to oppose the Welsh monopoly.

The Cornish Copper Company moved to Ventonleague on the Phillack creek in 1758 (see p. 111). The new Copperhouse smelter had between 20 and 30 reverberatory furnaces treating, with many remeltings, up to 6,000 tons of ore from the Camborne mines yearly. The weekly output of about 12 tons of copper was rolled into sheets with some bar and wire at Treloweth, St Erth. About 150 men were employed at the furnaces, but conditions were harsh and there was a high rate of early death from the arsenic fumes and heat. After 1800 the Copperhouse smelter declined steadily, not only from Welsh opposition but also from the economic disadvantage of lacking cheap and plentiful coal. The Cornish system of 'ticketing', the smelters' agents sampling ore stocks at mines at fixed dates to make their offers on tickets, gave the smelters a stranglehold on the copper trade which local entrepreneurs had no way of breaking. The wealth lost to Cornwall can be guessed from the output – between 1815 and 1905 7,300,000 tons of ore were raised yielding 568,000 tons of copper.

Of the tens of thousands engaged in winning Cornwall's immense wealth of metals only three small groups benefited richly: the lawyers who battened on the disputes arising in a complex industry, the mineral landlords and the smelters – Carlyle's 'Aristocracy of the Moneybag'. From the early seventeenth century with more than sixty known blowing houses at work, to the forty-three reverberatory furnace smelters which gradually superseded them from about 1700, and through the nineteenth century, the smelters had the rich end and the working tinners the poor end of the tin trade. D.B. Barton sums it up neatly, remarking ' . . . the profit in the industry came at the smelting rather than at the mining stage, in the refining and merchanting of the tin rather than its production as ore.'

Even when an effort was made by C.K. Vigurs in 1840 to form a co-operative of adventurers and miners to get a fairer return from smelting and marketing, the venture did not survive long in the face of opposition from the 'ring' of smelters. A correspondent to the *West Briton* (21.12.1938) estimated a loss to the great Wheal Vor near Godolphin Cross of £100,000 when operating its own smelter as 'they never possessed the secrets of distribution and were . . . in the hands of middlemen . . .' Some adventurers suffered similarly when they received 'dividends' in tin which they could only encash through the ring.

The ring was never a true cartel, but something very close. Barton again sums the position clearly: 'The trade in the metal was almost entirely in Cornish hands . . . whilst the smelters, by and large, were their own miners and their own merchants, and with a lucrative trade shared harmoniously amongst them competition was non-existent.' That they were 'their own miners' he emphasises: ' . . . they had a nose for tin, and, equally important, a nose for knowing where there was no tin. It is probably true to say that there was not a tin mine of any consequence . . . in which the smelters did not hold an important, and in many cases, a majority share.' And when mines began to fail smelters' names rarely, if ever, appear in the list of shareholders.

Barton also notes that: 'during the nineteenth century there was not a tin smelter in Cornwall who was not a banker.' L.C. Daubuz and Thomas Daniel of Truro, John Batten of Stable Hobba near Newlyn, R.R. Michell of Marazion, Williams Harvey and Co. of Mellanear, Hayle (who, like the Penpoll Tin Smelting Co. of Truro, moved to Liverpool when smelting failed in Cornwall) made their wealth in smelting, and were financiers to the county. Bolitho and Sons of Chyandour, Penzance, were not only smelters but already merchants of lime, cordage, tallow, charcoal and shipowners with a major share of the pilchard trade as well as becoming bankers of importance. To this day the cheques of Barclays Bank in Penzance and St Ives still carry the name of Bolitho's Bank as well.

Tin smelting started, as noted above, in small furnaces near the ore sources, but from the late seventeenth century to the twentieth 'white tin' came from larger works mainly built near the coinage towns. A large proportion of the ore raised and processed was smelted in the county in forty-three smelting houses working over various periods of time. Tin smelting by reverberatory furnaces was carried out at Newham, near Truro, as early as 1705, though they appear to have been used at Neath, in Wales, Polgooth near St Austell, and Treloweth, St Erth, before 1700. The many other smelters turned from the older method to the new, except for grain tin (tin heated almost to melting point and struck, when it fractured into small grains), before the eighteenth century was over, and continued with reverberatories until smelting ceased in the county.

Tin, like metals in other English mining fields, became subject very early to special controls. Though at first being treated and taxed like other villeins, the lowest order of medieval tenants, tinners were chartered in 1198 and 1201 and 1305 with a Crown-appointed Warden of the Stannaries with civil and criminal jurisdiction. Stannary courts dealt with all legal matters concerning tin mining, and a Stannary parliament passed laws which took precedence over national law, creating its own judiciary system and prisons (the latter in Launceston for Cornwall). Tinners were exempted from military service and market tolls; they could take fuel, divert streams for their workings, and could search freely through ('bounding rights') for tin in common land and in certain other areas. In return the smelted tin, export of 'black tin' being banned by Stannary law, was taxed by 'coinage'. This was a system under which cast tin blocks were taken to appointed towns at Midsummer and Michaelmas, or later every three months, a corner (French, 'coin') chiselled off, assayed and the block weighed to assess dues.

There were four Stannaries in Cornwall; Foweymore, roughly the Bodmin Moor area; Blackmoor, centred on St Austell;

Tywarnhaile, from St Agnes to Truro and Redruth; and the Kerrier-Penwith area. Five coinage towns were named, originally Bodmin, Lostwithiel, Liskeard, Truro and Helston, but later the first two were replaced by Penzance, and when coinage ended in 1838 Calstock and Hayle had been added. The coinage system together with the limited number of smelting houses gave the proprietors great economic control over the tin trade, and most of them also became bankers and Stannary financiers.

A view of the displays at the Royal Cornwall Museum in Truro, or the Royal Geological Society of Cornwall in Penzance will give an idea of the vast range of minerals that have been found in the County. Only a few have been of economic importance. Arsenic has been mentioned, lead and silver have been profitable in some areas, and iron, as at the Great Perran Iron lode, has been a worthwhile venture. Iron was even worked in Roman times on Trevelgue Head, Newquay. Wolfram for tungsten became valuable in the later nineteenth century, and zinc, manganese and antimony have all been worked. Cobalt for chinaware glaze from several ores and bismuth were also mined in commercial quantities. 'Tinners do also find little hopps of gold amongst their ore, which they keep in quills, and sell to the goldsmiths', Carew noted in 1602, and E.H. Davison and a friend paid for a holiday panning the Carnon stream in the 1930s. Gold in small amounts, first from alluvials in the Carnon and other valleys, has been made into a few items of jewellery, and has been reported from underground, in Wheal Jane for instance. Uranium ores have been raised from South Terras, Owles, Margery, Providence and Trenwith mines, the last providing the ore from which Marie Curie refined radium. There must still remain untouched huge underground resources, but the cost of reaching them, with all the problems left by earlier mining, may now be beyond reasonable consideration. Yet trial borings have still been made in very recent times. Sadder still is the rapidity with which the remains of this vast industry are vanishing; the pump houses, treatment plants and smelters are bulldozed, shafts hidden and waste dumps removed leaving no trace of the human endeavour once expended about the countryside. Modern needs must take priority, but not one mine complex remains complete in its old form to remind new generations of the hard and dangerous labour and the vast importance of the industry until recent times.

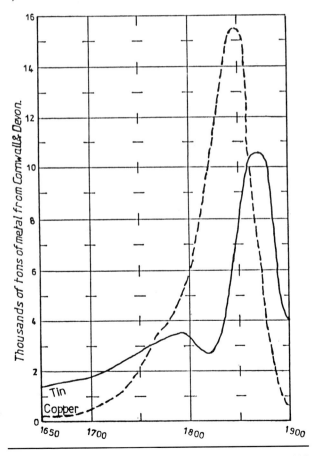

Graph showing rise and fall of tin and copper, 1650–1900

CHAPTER 7

China Clay

'Why,' replied the founder-master, "tis but the pot growan that comes from up yonder somewhere in the hills. 'Tis what we always use, and our fathers used it before us.'

Answer to a query from Wm. Cookworthy

ONLY one extractive industry has both survived into and expanded in the twentieth century, the winning of china clay and china stone which occur in greater or lesser amounts in the four large mainland Cornish granite bosses and one minor one. The industry is concentrated now in the Hensbarrow dome. The earliest use of china clay noted in the county was at the Romano-British village of Goldherring, Sancreed, where a hut was smoothly floored with raw clay, possibly brought from Leswidden, under Bartinney Hill. From comments by Cookworthy and others it appears that the clay was used to line smelting and other hearths, and china stone was used for building, for instance Probus church tower.

Its real importance only became obvious in the eighteenth century when growing trade with the Far East, and introduction of tea-drinking brought porcelain to European notice. The Chinese tea merchants usually included a small teapot and cup in their pack so that the buyer could check the quality. This kind of ware was unknown in the west, where only earthenware was made, usually of brown or red clays. Potters were spurred into a search for the materials from which the new body could be made. Inferior clays, alabaster, bone, soapstone from the Lizard and ground glass were tried, but only 'soft-paste' porcelain was produced as at Sèvres and Dresden. By 1710 a body closer to the 'hard paste' porcelain was achieved at Meissen and later at Vienna and Venice. In England it was only after 1740 that white china was made in potteries at Bow, Chelsea, Derby and Worcester and elsewhere, but still not the true porcelain. The Staffordshire potters were forced to look further afield for their clays, and the ball clays of Devon and Dorset were used for white earthenware.

The last step was made when two letters from a Jesuit priest, d'Entrecolles, in China, gave a specific account of the manufacture and materials of porcelain made in the Imperial Factory near Nanking (Nanjing), and the knowledge spread in Europe. William Cookworthy (1705-80) a young Quaker of Kingsbridge in Devon, self-educated in Latin and French, was apprenticed to a London Quaker apothecary, Sylvanus Bevan, a Fellow of the Royal Society, working in Lombard Street. In 1726 Bevan and Cookworthy set up as manufacturing chemists in Plymouth. Perhaps prompted by his brother Philip, mate on an East Indiaman, Cookworthy started searching for the 'petunse' (china stone) and 'kaolin' (china clay) described by d'Entrecolles. In 1745 he wrote to a surgeon friend in Penryn that he had met an American Quaker who had found those materials in Virginia and made china ware 'equal to the Asiatic' with them. Cookworthy was now a minister of the Quakers and for that reason and for business was travelling widely in Cornwall and Devon.

About 1748 he discovered china stone and china clay in Tregonning Hill, near Germoe, and later found 'immense quantities of both the Petunse stone and the Caulin' in the parish of St Stephens, near St Austell. It was not until 1768 that he was sufficiently satisfied with his experiments to take out a patent for his porcelain. With a young Quaker, Richard Champion, a factory was opened in Bristol and another in Plymouth. The Plymouth factory closed in 1770 and the patent transferred to

Champion, only to be modified in 1774 to free the materials for general use. Cookworthy had found the Tregonning Hill materials less satisfactory than those from St Stephen, and took a 99-year lease of a clay sett on Carloggas Moor from Thomas Pitt, later Lord Camelford.

Cookworthy's success brought a flood of the country's leading potters into Cornwall. Every 'sladdy bottom' – the waterlogged hollows on the moor – was searched, and by 1800 Josiah Wedgwood, Thomas Minton, Michael Kean of Derby China, the Royal Worcester Porcelain Co., Rose Blakeways of Coalport and Spode and Wolfe all had leases of clay ground and working pits, as well as independent clay merchants. Also, between 1750 and 1820 soapstone (steatite) from Gew Graze and other sites in the Lizard was being worked for the makers of 'soft paste' porcelain. Wedgwood considered establishing a major porcelain factory at the newly-created port of Charlestown, but the cost of the large quantities of coal necessary deterred him. After the Napoleonic war ended all the potters relinquished their leases, while retaining some financial interest, and the clay industry developed in largely local hands. One export outlet ceased completely in 1814, the 100 tons yearly (one twelfth of the whole product at that date) which was carted to Treyew Mill in Truro to mix with flour, probably less harmful than some of the adulterants used else- where in England. From about 1807 the finer clays were being used in the paper and cotton trades – about one fifteenth of the production of the mid-nineteenth century. Amalgamations reduced the number of independent producers through the nineteenth century, creating the way to the single concern of the twentieth, except for Goonvean and Rostowrack, near St Stephen-in-Brannel.

The shipping out of clay was ill-served by the coastline and the beaching of ships in coves for loading and refloating on suitable tides was dangerous. New ports had to be created.

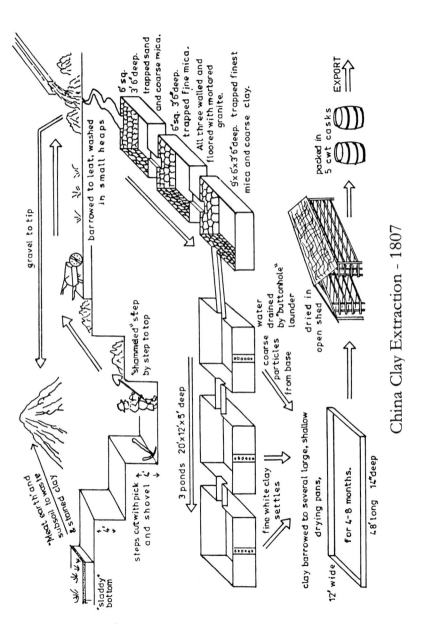

China Clay Extraction - 1807

gravel to tip

"Meat earth and subsoil to waste"
stained clay & sand

"sladdy" bottom

steps cut with pick and shovel

"shammeled" step by step to top

barrowed to leat, washed in small heaps

6 sq. 3'6" deep. trapped sand and coarse mica.

6' sq. 3'6" deep. trapped fine mica.

All three walled and floored with mortared granite.

9'x 6'x 3'6" deep. trapped finest mica and coarse clay.

3 ponds 20'x 12'x 5' deep

coarse particles from base

water drained by "buttonhole" launder

fine white clay settles

clay barrowed to several large, shallow drying pans,

12' wide
48' long
14" deep
for 4-8 months.

dried in open shed

packed in 5 cwt casks

EXPORT

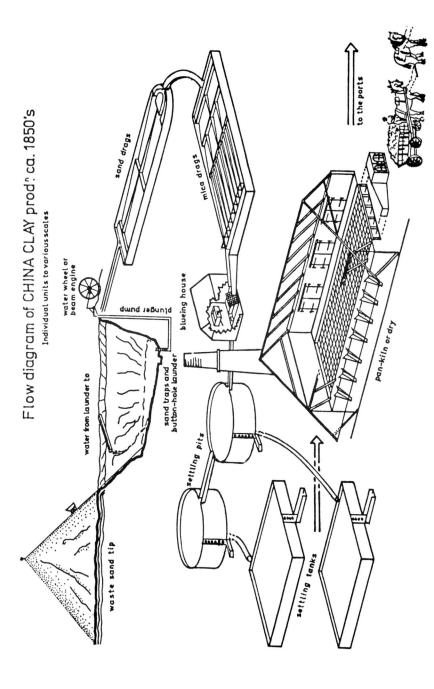

Flow diagram of CHINA CLAY prodⁿ. ca. 1850's

Individual units to various scales

waste sand tip

water from launder to

sand traps and button-hole launder

water wheel or beam engine

plunger pump

sand drags

mica drags

blueing house

settling pits

settling tanks

pan-kiln or dry

to the ports

Charlestown, with its dry dock and basin, built by Charles Rashleigh between 1791 and 1798 has been mentioned on p. 51; Pentewan was reconstructed in 1826 by Sir Christopher Hawkins and supplied by tramway from inland, but its short entrance canal was frequently choked; Fowey had a new quay built by Joseph Austen in 1813, but his greatest achievement was the creation of Par harbour between 1829 and 1840 on the un-promising flats at the Luxulyan River mouth, today a major port for clay traffic. Sea access was completed when Richard Lomax's new harbour at Newquay opened in 1833.

Much of the clay was casked and moved from moor to coast at first in heavy wagons over poor, rough roads, but as the trade increased and the new ports opened, tram and railway lines were laid, part of the Luxulyan River was canalized by Austen – now called Treffry – from Par to Pont's Mill, and a great leat and horse-drawn tramway built from an inclined plane at Pont's Mill 7, miles inland to Molinnis Moor. It included one of the finest of Cornish industrial monuments, the combined leat and tramway viaduct over the Luxulyan valley. Treffry bought Newquay har-bour and built a rail link to the clay country with an inclined plane from quayside to clifftop, opened in 1849. The working pits of the Hensbarrow area were linked by a network of railways to the ports, worked by horse, stationary engines and later steam locomotive. When the Cornwall Railway opened in 1859 rail connection with England was available. Improved and new roads were also made to serve the area.

In the other granite masses the main extraction was from the western side of Bodmin Moor where at least ten pits were worked, served by the line to Wenford Bridge. The Tregonning pits have been mentioned, in the small Germoe boss, but the great Carnmenellis mass and Carn Marth, both with proven kaolinisation, had no commercial pits. In the Land's End area pits at Towednack (Porthia), Tredorwin and under Bartinney

Hill, Leswidden and Bostraze, worked for limited periods into the twentieth century. Clay from the first named was moved by pipeline three miles to the 'dry' at St Erth station in its later working, and was favoured for paper making.

The changing processes of extracting clay from the raw 'growan' of the pit in the earlier and later nineteenth century are best described by the diagrams included here. The later method survived well into the twentieth century and can easily be followed at the Wheal Martyn Museum near St Austell.

Pliocene clays and sands from 400 feet up on St Agnes Beacon were used from early times for supporting miners' candles, for brick, glass and crucible making, and for the Truro potteries, the last survivor of which was Lake's Pottery on Chapel Hill. Similar clays and sands, remarkable for their fossil content, were taken from a pit at St Erth for pottery, a pit primarily opened for moulding sand for the foundries nearby. The clay was also used for puddling the new Penzance dock in 1880. The pit is now largely obscured by modern housing.

CHAPTER 8

Quarrying

. . . a great many little houses all of stone.
C. Fiennes

THE four main granite bosses and the lesser Germoe exposure have been mentioned above, but there are also a number of minor outcrops at Hingston Down and Kit Hill; Belowda Beacon and Castle-an-Dinas, St Columb; St Dennis on the edge of the Hensbarrow area; Carn Brea and Carn Marth near Carnmenellis; Cligga Head on the north coast; St Michael's Mount on the south; and, of course, the Scillies with the deep water Haig Fras reef sixty miles WNW of Scilly. It seems probable that all these sites are one continuous body at depth from Dartmoor in the east to the far west. The Cornish granite is mainly coarse-grained, often with felspar crystals several inches long, but the Land's End, Carnmenellis and Bodmin Moor highlands also have outcrops of intrusive fine-grain granite.

Early house building used the nearest suitable material to hand, only the wealthier houses using the reliable granite, even if not near at hand. Devonian slates and sandstones were extensively used also, and it is not unusual to find the source quarry near the building for which it was opened. In the moorland areas the loose surface granite 'moorstone' was used almost exclusively, even for the humblest farm outbuildings. After the early nineteenth century increased building had largely outrun that source, and quarried granite with its cubic cleavage was more widely used. In a country which had been denuded of timber by the mining interests it was used in ways not common elsewhere. Field hedges, tombs and tombstones, wayside and memorial crosses, all go back to the earliest days of Christianity, and some very much earlier. Granite now began to be used for finger-posts, farm troughs, gate posts and shed pillars, bridge beams and arches, stiles, field rollers, railway sleepers, roadside gutters and even engine bearings. Querns of granite go back to pre-historic time, and millstones, cider presses and crazing mills right on into the late nineteenth century. Paving slabs in both house and town are used over the same long span of time. The nineteenth century saw the expansion of granite quarrying, in the Mabe area for instance, for building, road kerbs and setts in the growing cities of the Industrial Revolution, and every granite area is pocked with quarries for local or export material.

Split granite at K. Spargo's Tolius Quarry, 1973

Tolius Quarry, 1973

Outstanding among the many quarry owners operating in Cornwall was the firm of William and John Freeman, stone merchants of Westminster, who came to dominate the granite industry from 1829. First buying from local agents to ship out almost all of the region's export, they opened Lamorna and other quarries in Penwith from 1829. Over the remainder of the century docks, breakwaters and lighthouses, bridges and the Thames Embankment, forts and foundations, public and commercial buildings, monuments and memorials, apart from the more humdrum items mentioned above, chiefly for Britain but also abroad, came through Freeman workshops from almost 130 quarries in all the granite areas. The stone was exported primarily from Penryn, the company headquarters, but also from Looe, Par, Wherrytown at Penzance and Lamorna. Some enormous pieces were quarried; one from Maen Quarry, Constantine, was 53 by 30 by 24 feet weighing 2,726 tons, another of 56 by 20 by 15 feet from Mabe of 1,250 tons, and Freemans shipped a 30-ton block for the base of a statue of Cromwell in Manchester.

It has already been noted that miners not unusually built their own homes, and where stone was not available 'cob' was used. This was a gritty clay mixed with straw or sometimes animal hair which, well whitewashed or tarred and soundly roofed was a sound, warm, long-lasting building material that almost any man could handle easily. The pits from which the cob material was taken are not often easy to trace.

The growth of industry demanded an improved road system, and granite provided an excellent material for the Turnpike Trust roads built from 1754 to 1863, and for the water-macadam roads of the nineteenth century. Though now deteriorating from weather and lack of maintenance many of those bye-roads surviving on the moors show how soundly they were built. Where the improved roads have come into heavy use, modernised and tarmacked, their foundations can be judged from the takepits strung along their length, often now used as parking and picnic spots for tourists.

Greenstone and other hard intrusive rocks, as well as granite, tarred for surfacing or as aggregate for concrete and as ballast for railroads, have been extensively quarried, but this development is mainly of the twentieth century.

Apart from the Bodmin Moor area most Cornish cottages, and sometimes larger houses, like those of Devon, were thatched well into the nineteenth century, though Celia Fiennes notes the slate roofs of Plymouth and Plympton in 1698. In Benjamin Martin's *The Natural History of England* (1759), in the chapter on Cornwall, he adds to his comments on St Michael's Mount this about Cornish choughs: 'they have the character of a thievish Bird, as they will carry from a Person's House whatever they can find to suit their Humour, even Coals, or anything on fire, they will carry away,and thereby endanger Houses, which are generally thatched in those parts; hence they become very obnoxious to the Neighbourhood where they much abound.' Whether Martin observed this, or received a fable for the unwary 'foreigner', one is left to wonder. The fire hazard posed by the many thatched houses in Truro was commented on in the *West Briton* of October 11th, 1811, and the danger to Crantock from a farm rick fire 'as the houses are almost all thatched' was reported in the *West Briton* on September 18th, 1812, when wetted winnowing sheets were spread over adjacent roofs.

Only the great houses, and the lesser ones near the quarrying areas, had slate 'heling stones' from as early as the Middle Ages. Carew wrote in 1602 ' . . . there are three sorts of slate . . . the first and best blue . . . is in substance thin, in colour fair, in weight light, in lasting strong, and generally carrieth so good regard as . . . great store is yearly conveyed by shipping both to other parts of the realm, and also . . . into Brittany and the Netherlands.' This must have applied to the Upper Devonian slate pit at Delabole, now one of the largest slate quarries in the world, and also the pits between there and the sea. Celia Fiennes had noted the 'black stone exceeding hard and glossy like marble' coming from 'Bole' on her journey out of Cornwall. There were many other quarries in mid and east Cornwall, as in the St Neot area of Middle Devonian age with the Carnglaze slate cavern, and Tresmarrow from which pit the *West Briton* of May 27th, 1814, reported a slate had been supplied of 84 square feet (7.8 sq.m) and 2 inches (5 cm) thick, with another in the quarry of 30 by nine feet (9 by 2.75m). William Marshall in 1796 observed 'at Launceston the houses are mostly faced with slates; some of them three or four feet square.' Some of the oldest sheds in Thomas Olver's china stone works at Tregargus, St Stephens, where utility not appearance was required, were roofed with slates up to 6 ft 6 in by 2 ft 6 in (1.98m by .76m) and less than $\frac{1}{2}$ in (1.2 cm) thick. The nineteenth century saw slate become the accepted standard for both domestic and industrial roofing, and frequently the cover for frame walls. Near some north coast ports Bridgwater pantiles were also used on industrial buildings. Thatch seems to have survived latest away from the mining areas.

Serpentine was widely quarried in the Lizard for building and for ornamental purposes, and though fracturing easily was alternated with granite as in Landewednack Church. Other hard rocks there as elsewhere in Cornwall were extracted for building or road making. The serpentinised picrite of Polyphant, near Launceston, and the blue-grey Cataclews elvan from near Trevose Head, both durable but readily worked, were widely used in church architecture in and beyond the county. The pink porphyritic granite with a matrix of black tourmaline from Luxulyan was used ornamentally, for instance in the large block from which the Duke of Wellington's tomb in St Paul's was made.

CHAPTER 9

Communications

I started for Bodmin to attend the County Railroad meeting . . . The Resolutions set forth the importance of the undertaking . . . and . . . of continuing Falmouth as a Packet Station.

Journal, October 29th,1839, Barclay Fox

Roads

CORNWALL, perhaps more than in England, was closely parochial, with travel difficult and largely limited to foot and horseback, and for most no farther than the nearest market town. When Celia Fiennes journeyed from Plymouth over the Cremyll Ferry and into Cornwall in 1698 she almost lost her horse in a pothole in a road near Looe. She observed that 'all over Cornwall and Devonshire they have their carriages on horses backes . . . I had the advantage of seeing their harvest bringing in, which is on horse's backe with sort of crookes of wood like yokes on either side.' And she noted of 'Redruth which is a little Market town; here they carry all their things on horses backes . . . little of size which they call Cornish Cavelys.' How necessary this mode of travel was she found again at Fowey; ' . . . a narrow stony town the streetes very close, and as I descended a great steep into the town soe I ascended one off it up a stony long hill . . . full of shelves and rocks . . . which . . . would have frighted me with its terribleness as the most in-accessible place as ever was . . . ' She did however note 'a broad coach rode which I have not seen since I left Exeter' as she went through narrow lanes from Tregony to Tregothnan, presumably the Truro-St Austell road.

To the end of the eighteenth century the bulk of the ore and coal moved in the county, as well as other goods, was carried by packhorse and 'moyle' (mule), thousands being used. A 'pare' (train) of mules could be as large as fifty or sixty animals but the usual team was twenty-one following a lead mare. Each carried two $1\frac{1}{2}$ cwt (76.2 kilos) leather or 'poldavy' (canvas) sacks slung over a special saddle. In earlier times a single 3 cwt sack was used, but the strain on the loaders making several trips a day with their 'pare' was too great. Borlase noted in the mid-eighteenth century that 'above five hundred, oftentimes a thousand animals at work' in Hayle. In the 1790s Portreath might receive as many as a thousand mule loads on a summer's day, but the unrepaired lanes became impassable even to mules in wet winter weather. Too often over-worked and inadequately fed, the bulk of these pack animals were imported from the West Indies, and as mining expanded their numbers far exceeded local supplies of fodder. Oats had to be imported from Ireland, adding to the cost of transport, and pushing the search for improved methods.

Almost a century after Celia Fiennes, William Marshall, riding through east Cornwall, wrote 'The roads are of stone and in some parts extremely well kept. The gates are few, and the tolls moderate. Toll roads are now formed between most or all of the market towns.' Worgan, who had travelled widely, went further in 1811 to assert (as noticed on p. 13), that 'No county affords a greater variety of wheel and other carriages than Cornwall. In most parts of the County may be met with the waggon, the wain, one and two-horse carts, the ox-butt, gurry-butt, slide and sledge.' The eighteenth century had indeed seen a widespread effort to improve communications, part perhaps of a social revival after the disasters of the Civil War, but mainly a reflection of the growing importance of metal mining. Henderson considered that 'It is probable that carriages and coaches became general in the time of Queen Anne [1702-14] for great improvements were made in the road system at that time.' This seems perhaps a little early for 'great improvements', but he adds 'By the reign of George III [1761-1820] we are in the thick of the Turnpike era ... ' The turnpike roads were to create a revolution in travel in the county and beyond. The first Turnpike Trust in the county was founded in 1754 at Truro and only expired in 1870. Between that first date and 1762 almost all the larger market towns had Trusts formed. Bodmin to Truro was added in 1769, and much later came the Hayle Causeway in 1825 and the Hayle-Redruth Trust in 1829. Previous to the opening of the Hayle Causeway traffic passed either round by St Erth bridge or over the sands to Lelant at low tide. The last turnpike to be built was from Penzance to St Just, only twenty-two years before all Trusts were abolished in 1885. An interesting tombstone by St Anthony-in-Meneage church is dedicated to 'Richard Roskuge who was killed when in the execution of his office of Surveyor of the Highways by a blow on his head with a biddaxe 14th August, 1797 aged 66 years.' At a date before any local newspaper, nothing more can be found about this sad incident.

Standards of road building naturally varied between Trusts, and even though costs were comparatively low they could be a heavy burden on the Trustees and must have modified their standards. An example of costs is shown in the St Ives Highways Disbursements Book for 1833-49. An improved access road into the town of 1,070 yards (980 m) cost the Borough £556 2s.1½d.) (£556.11) between Michaelmas 1834 and Lady Day 1838, an annual expense of £158 17s.7d. (£158.88), where it had previously been less than £100, and the work could not have been undertaken without a gift of £350 from local gentry. The town

Plate 78 shews the Road from Plymouth to Dartmouth.

Map after John Ogilby's *Britannia* of 1675

the Lands end

CORNWALL

Left strip:

to Pole Den
to Sehuan
Blow the Cold Wind
Peran-Arwothall 269
270
to Truo
cher R. 268
to Truo 267
to Penryn 6 m. thence to Falmouth 3
to Truo
to Mopas
to Penryn
to Kehstick 265
a Ferry 264
A
to Gerans 263
Philly
262 Debarth
Trenestron
to Sussel
261
to Trebourck
Prenargt to Gerans Trevan
259
to Trebarruck
258 to Truro
Vale R.
to Raskivei Truro
Tregouy
to Gerans
256 to Grampond
250 to Carveth to Grampond
255
to Fue Church to Pensance
254 Peruut
253 to Gerau Grampond
to St Tue

Middle strip:

S Michaels Mt
to Ludgfa 288
Market Jew or Merazion New or Fyen
to Helston 286 Henwor Henborn
Golsevyn Newelin St Hillary
to Ourla to St Ives
to Penryn to St Ives
284
to Truo
283
to Godolphin to Burvorge 282
to Gwynier
281 to St Ives
to Helston to Redrith
280 to S Ives
to Helston to Camburn 279
to Penryn to Redrith Hole R.
Cronvan
278
to Penryn to Camburn 277 to Redruk
to Helston 276
275 to Redruth
to the Blue Ston to Redruth to Truo
274
to Penryn
to Redruth
273 to Babule
272
to Sethians to Pole Day
to Penryn to Guinan 271

Right strip:

Treville
300 Senan
Trua 299
298
Raubert Brevethel
to Barnavel 297 to Penrose
Poudrea St Burien
296 to Carvew Lea
297 Tregedath
to Travels 294 Sancred
to La more to Kirthier to Kiry Moor to Alverton Moor
293 St Paule to Kirdino
Chur 292 Treveneth
Newland Laregon
291 to Alverton to the North Sea
Pen-sance
Mounts Bay 289 Gulvall

rate levy was even assisted by the sale of dung, though only by a matter of shillings. Hand-broken stone for the work cost from 10d.(4p approx.) to 1s.8d. (8p approx.) though usually 1s.(5p) a cartload. Labourers were paid 1s.6d. to 2s.(7½p to 10p) a day, mainly the latter, and masons paved the road at 7d. (3p approx.) a yard.

In a county where good road stone was readily available it was the care taken in breaking stone to the best size that governed the quality of the road, so it is not surprising that when John Loudon Macadam was posted to Falmouth in 1798 as a victualling officer he was to test his new theories on a local road, the turnpike between Truro Workhouse and Kiggan Mill near Tresillian, still open though long since bypassed. Apparently it was an example quickly learned, for the *West Briton* of November 8th, 1822 reported that 'the turnpike roads in the vicinity of Truro are certainly kept in a much better state of repair than in many parts of the county; this is the result of . . . the practice of breaking the stones . . . to a much smaller size than heretofore; by which the surface is more equal and safe, and also more durable than where larger stones are made use of.'

The costs of maintenance were met by tolls; for instance at Truro in 1817 all draught animals with vehicles were charged 6d. (2½p), other beasts of burden 2d. (1p approx.), herds of cattle 1s.3d. (6p approx.) per score, and droves of calves, sheep etc. 8d. (3p approx.) per score. Some Trusts also imposed a ban on vehicles with wheel rims less than 6 inches (15 cm approx.) wide, as narrow rims were thought to damage the roads. The toll-houses, with their three-faced frontage, which once barred the roads to all but the Royal Mails can still be found scattered plentifully round the country, a good guide to the old Trust roads.

Henderson says in his *Old Cornish Bridges* that Sir Reginald Mohun of Hall near Fowey kept a coachman in 1637, but Noall says 'the first coach . . . owned by a Cornishman belonged to the Hawkins family of Trewinnard, St Erth, . . . about 1700.' It may have arrived in the county much later, and is now in the Royal Cornwall Museum. There are several reports in the eighteenth century of the whole population of towns turning out to watch the passage of a wheeled vehicle, but after 1800 there was certainly no such novelty. From about 1760 post-chaises, two- or four-horse closed carriages, were beginning to be used in many parts of the county but cost up to 10d.(4p) a mile. About 1790 the first stage-coach, from Exeter through Bodmin to Truro, was established, soon to be followed by other public and stage-coach services. By the standards of the day travel was far from cheap; Hooper and Co.'s coach in 1799 charged inside passengers £1 4s.0d. (£1.20) from Torpoint to Falmouth, and 12s. (60p) to outside passengers, with a baggage allowance of 12 lb (5.5 kilos approx.) for each traveller. The first Royal Mail coach was established in 1806, running from Plymouth to Falmouth. The new roads and new vehicles, however, did not bring total comfort to the traveller. Many coaches had leather blinds, not windows in the doors, and 'the atmosphere', as Southey describes, 'was neither fresher nor more fragrant than that of a prison.' Even with improved springing and smoother surfaces the motion was not always agreeable. For the outside passengers, facing all that the weather could bring, winter travel could be a nightmare, and upsets, particularly in night travel, were not unknown. Even as late as 1836 James Halse MP and his lady coming from London found it preferable to change to the *Herald* steamer at Bristol to come on to Hayle on their way to St Ives. J. Allen in 1856 described the coaches from Torpoint to Liskeard as 'clumsy, and drawn by four heavy horses at a slow pace of four miles an hour over fearful roads and hills,' but not all travellers were so critical.

One of the great spurs to improved coaching was the choice

of Falmouth as the home port for the Packet Service from 1689 to 1852 (except for November 1810 to January 1811) with sailings to Lisbon, the Mediterranean, West Indies, North America and Brazil. In the 1820s some forty services were sailing from the town which, wrote Southey in 1802, was a continual bustle of passengers arriving to embark, perhaps with a long wait, or disembarking and in haste to be on their way home. He quotes an inscription on the wainscot of a Truro inn: 'Thanks to the Gods another stage is past', a comment perhaps less on the speed than on the quality of the journey. For the poor, the few who went far afield, there were Russell's Waggons leaving Falmouth at noon on Monday and reaching London on Saturday. These had been established in 1801, with a warehouse at Back Quay, Truro, to carry bullion, diamonds and other valuable packets, and had an armed military guard. The poor traveller had company and safety on his long walk, and in summer could sleep in the shelter of the waggon.

Water-macadam was the standard method of surfacing the main highways and often lesser roads, and though now hidden may be traced when roads are trenched. From the 1820s on, the larger towns followed industrial examples and had gasworks built. Tar, as a by-product, became readily available with a market in the shipping world and building, but no reference has come to hand on the use of tar-macadam. There must have been some nineteenth century roads using that improved surface, perhaps only privately. The dusty country road remained well into the twentieth century, and the granite setts which paved many town roads survive in some places to this day.

The story of roads cannot be left without mention of the Cornish pioneer Sir Goldsworthy Gurney (1793-1875) of Wadebridge and later Bude. When young he had seen Trevithick's road carriage and they corresponded for many years. He experimented with the same idea from 1825, using a tubular boiler and coke for fuel, and in July 1829 a 12 h.p. coach made a successful run from London to Bath at 6 m.p.h. In 1831 a regular service was run between Cheltenham and Gloucester. Though his vehicles were proved viable and safe, opposition from public and vested interests led to punitive tolls being imposed, and the steam carriage vanished in favour of railways.

Canals

WHILE the roads were being improved the 'Canal Mania' which had swept England also touched Cornwall despite the unpromising terrain. The first to be cut was a widening of the Angarrack stream along the south side of the Phillack inlet in 1769, to enable ships of up to seventy tons to reach the Cornish Copper Company works at Copperhouse, half a mile from the Hayle estuary. Water-gates at the inner end of the canal impounded the stream which could be flooded out to clear silt

Pentewan basin and canal, with narrow-gauge railway and minerals tub visible

from the channel. A weir and lock gates were added in 1788 to close off the outer end of the creek at high tide, and opened at low tide to flush clear the sea channel and sand-bar in the bay for larger vessels. The dock by the works was also penned by lock-gates to avoid stranding ships at the wharves.

The Hayle canal may not have been the first, for John Edyvean as a boy had worked in the Carclaze tin mine near St Austell where, twenty-two fathoms underground, a canal half a mile long was discovered in 1852. In the 'Report of the Penzance Natural History and Antiquarian Society it was thought not to have been seen for at least 120 years. There were 16 flat-bottomed boats, six feet long, on it. Whether he saw it and was inspired or not, in later life he proposed a number of canal schemes, including one to run the length of England, and in 1773 he embarked on a canal of his own near Newquay. This was in two parts, one starting at Lusty Glaze cove with a steep inclined plane up which tubs of sand were hauled. On the cliff above there was a boat basin, now a car park, and another passing basin in what is now the yard of a nearby inn. The canal ran inland on about the 100 foot contour for nine miles, but most is now obscured. The second part started above the cliff of Trenance Point at Mawgan Porth and was cut inland for three miles to Whitewater farm. Some cargoes of sand for fertilizer were carried, but the canal does not seem to have worked for long and is not shown on the OS 1-inch map of 1809.

The only long canal in the county was authorised in 1819 to run from the beach at Bude inland by Marhamchurch, Hobbacott, Red Post and Venn to its created water source, the Tamar Lake near Alfardisworthy. Its primary trade was to be shell-sand fertilizer inland and farm produce out. A branch from near Lana ran east near Chilsworthy and north of Holsworthy to Blagdonmoor, over 130 m above sea level. A second branch ran south from near Red Post to the Tamar at Bridgerule and beside the river to Druxton Wharf near Eggbear, thirty-five and a half miles of canal in all completed by 1826. Much of this latter branch is still shown on the OS landranger series, but a glance at that map shows deep valleys across the routes as well as great changes in height. Earlier proposals in the eighteenth century had included the use of trucks on inclined planes involving cargo transfer put forward by Edyvean, and for a lock system by Smeaton, but these were abandoned.

The scheme finally put under way in 1819 was for a tub-boat narrow canal, under the direction of James Green, Surveyor of Bridges and Building for Devon. He adapted a system, advocated by the American engineer Robert Fulton, of inclined planes with haulage provided by water-ballast buckets dropping down wells for power on the long slopes, and water-wheels on the shorter hauls. Six inclines were used on the canal, more than on any other, and the Hobbacott incline was the longest ever built. At Hobbacott there was a double railway over the 935 ft (285m) long slope, rising 225 ft (68.5m), the rails running into the canal at each end. The two buckets, each 10 ft (3 m) in diameter and 5 ft 6 ins (1.7m) deep, held 15 tons (15.25 tonnes) of water, descending the 225 ft wells alternately on to stakes which opened plugs to empty them by tunnel into the lower canal. They hauled the tub-boats up the slope in four minutes. If the bucket chains broke there was a 16 hp steam engine as standby. The Marhamchurch incline, similarly worked, was 836 ft long (255 m) with a 120 ft rise (36.5 m), the others between 50 and 60 ft (15.25 and 18.25 m) and worked by water-wheel.

At Bude a new breakwater was built at the same time as the canal work started at several points, together with a large locked basin to hold a number of sea-going ships as well as the barges and tub-boats. It still remains in use. A narrow-gauge railway ran down to the beach from the basin for trucks to haul sand up for the tub-boats. These latter were 20 ft (6 m) long, 5 ft 6 ins

(1.7 m) wide, with a draught of only 1 ft 8 ins (.51 m), and fitted with wheels for the inclines. They carried about 4 tons. The canal worked until 1891, carrying between 30 and 50 thousand tons of sand yearly, as well as other cargoes, almost to the end, but was never really profitable. Only the section from Tamar Lake to Venn remains open, the water then being piped to supply the Bude area.

As the Bude canal neared its opening, a new canal was started in 1825 at Liskeard and opened in 1828 running over five miles from Moorswater below the town and beside the East Looe river to the deep water of the Looe inlet. Like the others it was designed originally to bring sea-sand and limestone for fertilizer inland and farm produce out, but when copper was found on Caradon Moor in the 1830s it provided the last stage for the ore carted down from the mines. As the mines expanded the Liskeard and Caradon Railway replaced the waggons, and in 1860 the canal was replaced by a railway to Looe.

The tiny Pentewan canal, opened in 1826 and closing in 1919, has already been mentioned on p. 95 as has the one and half mile Treffry or Par canal opened in 1847. The two-mile Fowey to Lostwithiel canal from the tidal head of the Fowey ria, opened in 1828 to carry clay and minerals, was also replaced by railway in 1869.

There were many abortive proposals for canals in the county and they are included here for interest. Colonel Trevanion had an Act of Parliament to build sluices on the Fal to bring shipping to Grampound Bridge in 1667. Three schemes to join the Camel and Fowey rivers were made; first by Trehawke in 1755, by William Borlase later with Rennie as his adviser, by Robert Fraser in 1794, and one mentioned by Brunel in his journal for March 1825. In 1780 canals from Portreath to North Downs, and from Restronguet to Bissoe or Twelveheads were proposed, without sufficient support despite the great needs of the flourishing copper mines. Another from Hayle to Carwynnen Bridge in 1801 for the other end of the copper mining area suffered similarly, as did a canal for the lead ore of Old Wheal Rose to the Gannel in the 1820s. A further large area which it was hoped might be served by canal was the Clowance-Wendron mining complex where, in 1796, the great American engineer Robert Fulton planned a waterway using parts of the St Erth, Cober and Gweek valleys, winding its way through a rich assortment of mines to the Helford River. The prospectus was carefully drawn up for a practicable venture, but again support was lacking.

To avoid the dangerous rounding of Land's End a canal from Hayle to Marazion was mooted in 1834 but, like the rest, could not raise enough public interest in an age when steam power and railways were more promising.

Railways

CORNWALL at the beginning of the nineteenth century was the busiest and richest mining field in the world, naturally attracting the finest engineering minds, native and visiting, to the solution of its problems. Horse- or man-drawn tramways of wood or stone had been used in many parts of Britain from the early seventeenth century, and of iron plate or rail with flat or flanged wheels on the wagons from the second half of the eighteenth, so it is not surprising that, as the demands and costs of mule transport grew, a tramway should be considered for the booming Camborne mines. First proposed by Lord de Dunstanville in 1806, and started in 1809 with George Fox and John Williams, a tramway was built from the new eastern basin of Portreath harbour up the valley, on to North Downs mine (OS survey 1809, published 1813, sheet 31) and through Scorrier to Poldice mine, with a branch to Treskerby mine. One hundred mules were advertised for in July 1811, but the line probably came into use in March 1812. Cast-iron L-shaped plates, three feet long, with a gauge of three feet made the track, and the line continued operating until North Downs and Treskerby closed in 1855, though occasional use for coal and other goods was reported in the *West Briton* as late as June 1885. Its small, open Directors' truck survives in the keeping of the Trevithick Society, now on display in the Royal Cornwall Museum in Truro.

This was still an ancient technology but the new was already arriving. In 1784 William Murdoch had made a steam-powered model locomotive, and in 1801 Richard Trevithick drove a high-pressure steam carriage up Camborne Hill. In 1802 another small loco designed by Trevithick was driven on rails at Coalbrookdale, and in 1804 his full-scale engine moved ten tons of iron and seventy men over nine miles on the Pen-y-daran tramroad. The age of steam traction was still a few years ahead, to be developed by others, but Cornwall had been the seed-bed.

Cornwall's first railway was the Redruth-Chasewater opened in 1825 with a four foot gauge, running nine miles from Redruth to Restronguet Creek (though the Chasewater branch was never built), horse-drawn until locomotives were introduced in 1854. It closed down in 1915. A light railway probably of four foot gauge connected St Austell with the little port of Pentewan in 1829, carrying clay down by gravity, and returning trucks by horse. It used locomotives from 1873 on a gauge of 2 ft 6 ins (.762 m) until it closed in 1919, but parts of its course, and even rails at the loading bay by the canal, can still be seen (1987).

The first steam railway opened on July 4th, 1834, when the Bodmin and Wadebridge line opened with the 'Camel' loco-motive, designed at the Cornishman Henry Taylor's Neath Abbey Ironworks in South Wales. It was not just a mineral line but carried passenger traffic also from Wadebridge to Wenford

Bridge with branches to Bodmin and Ruthernbridge, but remained isolated until it was linked to the Great Western at Bodmin Road in 1887. Later, in 1895, it was also joined to the North Cornwall Railway at Wadebridge.

Later lines were still opened as horse-drawn ventures, probably because they were primarily for ore, coal and stone haulage with passengers imposing themselves willy-nilly. The 4 ft 8½in gauge (1m 43.5 cm) Hayle Railway, opening in stages from December 1837, used horses from Hayle through Phillack to an incline at Angarrack where steam power hauled the trains up to a locomotive for the line to Redruth; stationary engine assisted on inclines at Penponds and the branch line to Tresavean mine. A branch from Redruth to Portreath required a long incline with a stationary engine for the drop to the valley bottom, where again horses were used round the dock. The line on the high ground was raised on an embankment which can be traced over considerable lengths; the inclines are still landmarks and a small three-span stone bridge of 1837 survives over the stream at Phillack. In 1843 the line began a passenger service and was one of the first to run excursion trains, from the mining towns to the Hayle beaches. In 1846 the line was taken over by the West Cornwall Railway and realigned to replace the inclines with viaducts, including over Hayle.

Three other mineral lines opened in the 1840s; for the growing china clay industry Joseph Treffry joined his canal at Pont's Mill to Bugle in 1842 with its magnificent rail and leat viaduct over the Luxulyan river, the line later extended to Fowey including a surviving short tunnel. In 1849 Treffry added a line from Newquay harbour with an inclined tunnel and a timber viaduct over the Trenance valley running inland to St Dennis, with a branch to East Wheal Rose. Both used horse traction, and water-wheel power on the inclines, and used the standard 4 ft 8½ in. gauge (1m 43.5 cm). In 1844 the Liskeard and Looe

Portreath railway incline, 1934

Union Canal at Moorswater was connected to the Cheesewring quarries and Caradon mines by a standard gauge line on granite sleepers, moving stone and ores down by gravity and returning wagons by horses. In 1860 the traffic had so increased that the line was extended to Looe in the south, and to Tokenbury east of Caradon Hill, and locomotives were introduced. The Looe section carried passengers from 1879, though they had been allowed in mineral wagons or coaches from much earlier.

1846 and 1847 saw two more lines authorised which were to be of far-reaching future importance: the West Cornwall Railway and the Cornwall Railway. The Cornwall Railway work started at Truro, opposed by riots prompted by fears of food shortage, in August 1847, after considerable differences of opinion on its route, and very soon met financial difficulties, bringing the work to a halt. Meantime, Brunel having been appointed engineer to both railways in place of a Captain Moorsom, and despite his preoccupation with the South Devon Railway, the West Cornwall was started in 1850. It was of standard 4 ft $8\frac{1}{2}$ in gauge but with bridges and embankments on a scale to take broad gauge if required, with V-shaped Barlow rails which later had to be changed. The first passengers were carried from Penzance to Redruth in March 1852 and to Truro in August. Work restarted on the Cornwall line in that year and the English connection was completed with the opening of the Royal Albert tubular suspension bridge over the Tamar on May 4th, 1859. The bridge chains had been made at the CCC Copperhouse foundry for Brunel's temporarily aborted Clifton bridge, but were repurchased for use at Saltash.

The line needed thirty-four viaducts to Truro, plus nine west of Truro, and the Falmouth branch, completed in 1862, a further eight, as well as many, mostly short, tunnels. The bridges, except the lowest which were timber, were on stone piers with a fan of pairs of four pine beams thirty feet plus in length supporting the track bed. From the 1870s they were replaced by masonry or iron, though the last to be rebuilt lasted to July 1934 at Collegewood, Penryn. The West Cornwall added a third rail at the 7ft $\frac{1}{4}$in broad gauge (2m 13cm) in 1866, the last broad gauge line being the St Ives branch in 1877, much of the WCR having three rails for both gauges for many years. The difficulties caused by Brunel's gauge at the junctions with Stephenson's 4ft 8$\frac{1}{2}$in. were so great that the Great Western system had to be changed to the national system. The section from Exeter to Penzance was re-laid in two days after May 20th, 1892. The old semi-isolation of Cornwall was gone for good, and Wilkie Collins was one of the last to be able to 'ramble beyond railways'. Though mining was failing, agriculture at least could reach better markets and the fishery new ones. Tourism would eventually provide some replacement income for other lost wealth. The detached early mineral lines, too, were joined to the through track, with improved passenger connections to Fowey and Newquay in 1876 by the Cornwall Minerals Railway, and Helston in 1887, the first and last now gone. Finally the neglected north Cornwall was opened by the extension of the North Cornwall Railway, part of the L&SWR, from Okehampton to Launceston in 1886, Wadebridge in 1895 and Bude in 1898, though now closed and dismantled since 1967. Perranporth was served from Chasewater on the main line in 1903, and from the Newquay branch in 1905, the start of the change to tourism.

CHAPTER 10

The Foundries and Engineering

Rode to Perran . . . to be present at the casting of a great cylinder . . .
such an impetuous torrent of white-hot fiery flop rushing from the lips
of 2 furnaces through 2 channels to opposite sides of the mould.
Journal, May 7th, 1842, Barclay Fox

THE smith was always a key figure in country life, providing the
farm tools and minor domestic items of wrought iron and small
castings. In the second half of the eighteenth century, as mines
sank deeper, and water-powered pumps became less adequate,
steam power in the form of Newcomen (as early as 1716) and
Boulton and Watt engines (from 1777) was introduced from
England. Their parts were manufactured at Neath Abbey Iron
Works in Wales, Boulton's Soho Works in Birmingham, Darby
or Wilkinsons at Coalbrookdale in Shropshire, or Carron
Ironworks in Scotland.

Engineers such as Jonathan and Josiah Hornblower, Edwin
Bull and William Murdoch came into Cornwall to erect and
maintain first the Newcomen and then the Watt engines needed
by an ever-growing number of mines. Like John Smeaton, who
greatly increased the efficiency of the Newcomen engine he built
at Chasewater, and in face of the intransigence of James Watt,
they improved and developed steam power, and settled in the
county beside the local men who were adding their ideas. After
1800 when Watt's patent expired these men were free to develop
their ideas, and their engineering needs were met in the nineteenth century by at least thirty brass and iron foundries manufacturing everything from massive steam pumps, steam engines

121

and water-wheels to gearings, domestic stoves, shovels and nails. Some enterprising village smiths, like John Harvey of Carnhell Green, graduated to build the heavy engineering foundries the county needed, and the engines they made were to win international use and fame.

The story of the great contribution made from Cornwall to the Industrial Revolution centres above all at Hayle with Harvey and Co. and the Cornish Copper Company Foundry (later known as Sandys, Carne & Vivian) at Copperhouse, and at Devoran with Fox and Co.'s (later Williams') Perran Foundry. From 1800 on a majority of the pumping engines supplied to mines in Cornwall came from those three foundries, and many more were shipped to mining fields all round the world from Ireland to Australia. One estimate credits 1,250 engines to the three out of the 1,550 made in the county.

One of the first successful steam locomotives, Trevithick's, with parts made at Harvey's, was tested in 1801, but it was his high-pressure boiler made for him by Nicholas Holman at Pool, near Camborne, about 1812, which made it possible for the Cornish Engine to reach its pre-eminence in the world's mining fields and for pumping water throughout the nineteenth century and into the twentieth.

The Cornish Copper Company was floated in 1755 by G. Johns, engineer, the Rev. J. Trevenen and J. Vivian, merchant, and the works opened at Carn Entral, a mile east of Camborne church. Local ore was bought and smelted with coal shipped into Hayle. Experience showed that three times the weight of coal to copper ore was needed, and the only transport from the sea was by mule train so a move nearer to the port was made in 1758. With the land about the junction of the two branches of the sheltered but sand-plagued Hayle estuary in other entrepreneur's hands, the CCC settled at Ventonleague near the head of the eastern inlet. A canal to the estuary was cut in 1769,

Cornwall's first, with dock gates near the foundry and sluice gates at the western end to pound water for release on the ebb tide to flush the channel to the sea. This action was to be one critical factor in the long battle with the Harveys mentioned below.

Copper production continued to 1819 when, in the face of Welsh smelters' competition, the company ended it as its main business. With mines supplies as an important, and monopoly, subsidiary trade, that business and the import of coal and timber and export of copper ore continued. The company also began producing iron castings, and in the following fifty years it grew to manufacture at least 350 Cornish engines by various engineers for county mines and abroad and waterworks in London, as well as iron ships and ships' engines, chains, gasworks and lighting equipment, water-wheels, machinery for roadworks and ore crushing, the first locomotive for the Hayle-Redruth railway, bells for nine Cornish churches and their own for the foundry (now in Penlee House Museum) and a host of items on demand. To meet the necessary expansion the works were extended westward beside the creek. Chains made by the CCC to Brunel's design for Hungerford Suspension Bridge (1845) in London were later re-used for his Clifton Suspension Bridge when it was completed in 1864. The chains designed by Brunel for the Clifton bridge and made by the CCC supplied nearly half the links for the Albert Bridge in Plymouth (1859), and the company also provided chains for Lambeth Bridge. The decline in mining and trade in general, plus the death of partners, forced the winding-up of the company in 1869. Another Copperhouse industry from 1848 was James Pool's perforated iron screens, taking over much of the CCC works, and surviving for three-quarters of the twentieth century.

In 1779 John Harvey moved from his smithy at Carnhell Green, despite lack of capital, to set up a small foundry with a reverberatory furnace and boring mill under the Carnsew hill beside the shallow Penpol stream flowing into the Hayle estuary. He even undertook very specialised work, for instance casting the nine-hundredweight tenor bell for Stithians Church in 1790, still in use. In this he was not alone for a bell for St Buryan was locally cast in 1738, and Christopher Pennington at Mabe had cast Constantine's Great Bell in 1744. In 1780 the creek was deepened to bring vessels up to the works. Success led him to import coal and pig-iron in his own ship which he kept busy with cargoes for the neighbouring mines. This competition led the CCC merchanting monopoly into a vicious and sometimes violent trade war with the Harvey family which was not ended until a prolonged law suit (turning on the change of course of the Penpol stream by the CCC canal sluicing) gave judgement to the Harveys in 1831. Their right to the Penpol channel and wharves was confirmed and the bar to expansion removed. The foundry company remained as mine and building merchants also, and ship owners and builders. Now they became general store-keepers, furnishers and drapers, innkeepers, farmers, millers, bakers, ropemakers with timber and coal yards additionally, and tin smelting had been added from 1816 to 1824. Meantime the foundry made anything required in metal from nails and wire to gas lighting systems and massive steam engines.

John Harvey's sixteen-year-old son Henry joined the firm in 1791, and was to be its driving force up to his death in 1850, ably assisted until 1828 by the skilled craftsman William West. In 1797 Richard Trevithick, Cornwall's most inventive engineer, married Henry's sister Jane, and the foundry made the cast parts for his first steam road carriage in 1801 and 1802, a steam rock drill for Plymouth breakwater work and other machines; but it was for their Cornish mine pumps that the foundry is most renowned.

The first steam pump was made at Harvey's in 1792, probably

a Newcomen, but it was not until Trevithick applied his new high-pressure boiler and the expansive power of steam to a re-used 24 in (61 cm) cylinder at Wheal Prosper Mine at Gwithian in 1812, all the necessary adapting parts being made at Harvey's, that the future triumph of the firm was made possible. This was the first true Cornish Engine, and the forerunner of the five hundred which were to come from the foundry, a high proportion of the county's output. A series of fine, powerful engines, such as the Austen's at Fowey Consols of 1833, culminated in the Leeghwater, Cruquius and van Lijnden pumps, built between 1843 and 1849 to drain the Haarlemmer Meer in Holland. They were the largest steam pumps ever made, using the compound engine system unsuccessfully patented by Jonathan Hornblower in 1781. The design produced by Harvey's had a high pressure 84 in (2m 13.5cm) cylinder contained within a massive 144 in (3m 66cm) low pressure cylinder working eleven beams to the pumps. When the Leeghwater engine, with some small parts made by Fox's Perran foundry, was proved successful, raising 112 tons of water 10 feet per stroke, two more were ordered. The Cruquius engine was entirely Harvey's product and remained working until 1933, and is now preserved. Fox's foundry was commissioned for the van Lijnden engine but the cylinder was cast by the CCC.

Under Nicholas Harvey the second half of the century saw the building of Porthleven harbour and more iron steamship building, while the foundry offered an almost total supply of mine equipment from any size of pump to shovels. Apart from mining a wide range of domestic supplies was produced, including farm tractors, cooking ranges, cast metal window frames and fire irons. There seems to have been no metal work too large or too small that would not have been made. The grist milling, drapery and grocery businesses were disposed of to J.H. Trevithick, son of the inventor, in 1851, but the other merchanting was retained.

Nicholas died in 1861 but was ably succeeded from the Harvey and West family members on the board, carrying on the firm until, in 1875, it was able to purchase its failing old enemy the Cornish Copper Company.

The last great undertaking of the foundry was for the Great Western Railway's Severn Tunnel. When the trial heading had been partly driven in 1879 it was flooded by the Great Spring. Cornish engines had been ordered from Harvey's at the start of work and were erected after the flood, allowing the tunnel to reach near completion by 1883, when the spring again burst in. Three more engines from closed mines and a new one built at Hayle were brought in to drain the tunnel and in 1885 double broad gauge lines were laid and the first trial run made. Soon the brick tunnel linings threatened to give way under the spring pressure. A new shaft was sunk to receive the spring and six large Cornish engines plus two for other shafts were ordered from Harvey's. By the end of 1886 the Sudbrook Pumping Station was moving 23 to 30 million gallons (104,328,000 to 136,080,000 litres) of water a day and the tunnel was open. It continued so with the same engines well into the 1960s when they were superseded by more modern power units.

Cornish mining was coming to an end and though mining equipment, particularly for South Africa, was still exported, and the steamship *Ramleh* (3,800 tons) (3,740 tonnes) built, the foundry ceased to be profitable and was finally wound up in 1904. Only the merchanting continued.

The third of the great trio of engineering foundries opened in 1791 beside the tidal Perran Creek, seven miles from the open sea of Falmouth Bay, by the Quaker Fox family. In the following year they added coal, iron and copper smelting interests at Neath in South Wales. Though they were trade competitors there seems to have been friendly co-operation between the Foxes and Harveys, both foundries producing a very similar wide range of goods. The Williams' Perran Foundry (successor to the Foxes after 1857) catalogue of *c*. 1870 carries at least sixteen of the same woodblocks as the Harvey catalogue of 1884, with only the names changed. By the closing down of the foundry in 1879 it had made about 400 Cornish engines. The Fox family continued the timber side of their business, which finally became part of the Harvey concern in the 1950s.

These were the giants, but as mentioned above there were many smaller concerns adding their output and expertise, about 300 Cornish engines from what were village industries for instance. It was Nicholas Holman at Pool who made Trevithick's first high-pressure boiler, and others of his family who, in Camborne, were to become world renowned for their rock drills. There were the Bartles of Camborne and Illogan, E.T. Sara of Camborne, Sara and Sons of Tolgus, Redruth, and later Nicholas Holman at Nancherrow, St Just, making boilers, the Charlestown Engineering Co., Irons Brothers and Oatey and Martin of Wadebridge, Visick and Son of Devoran, the Calstock Tamar Ironworks and others, sometimes only brought to mind by roadside gratings or inspection covers. Such are the dwindling reminders of one of the rich wellsprings of the Industrial Revolution.

CHAPTER 11

The Supporting Trades and Services

> . . . they will maintain the state of the world, and all their desire is
> in the work of their craft.
>
> .   Ecclesiasticus

THE farmer was supported by a range of craftsmen, primarily by
the local smiths and by cartwrights and wheelwrights. Shoeing
of his draught animals, oxen, horses or mules, was a regular need
and other calls on the smith were for the repair and tempering of
his tools, made by the smith in the first place to the individual
demands of the job and the man. Tools for local trades and
individual workers can be seen in many farm museums; at the
Wayside Museum, Zennor, for instance.

Horse-drawn vehicles, the product of another group of skilled
tradesmen, were also governed by local conditions and individual needs, though they became less so as the roads of the region
improved. Their workshops are rarely traceable now, though a
clue may sometimes show in the form of a large diameter
'millstone', often granite, but smooth surfaced with a central
hole on which a wheel was fitted with its iron tyre.

In a few places on the map of Cornwall the name Tuckingmill
appears, indicating the site of former fulling mills, for, like much
of rural England, there was a homespun cloth industry for those
who could not afford the finer serges and woollens of Devon
and Yorkshire or costly imported fabrics. There was a serge and
flannel mill in the Kennal Vale, Ponsanooth, until the third
quarter of the nineteenth century, and a broadcloth weaving mill
was working in Camelford from November 1811, using merino

wool from Cornish sheep-runs. Near Menheniot there were three- or four-storey woollen factories, the first 120 feet long and 50 feet wide, far removed from the cottage industry of earlier times, and a smaller three-storey factory 'on the latest improved Yorkshire plan' was operating near Ladock. A machine-spinning factory operated in Grampound in the first quarter of the century.

There must have been many other factories, large or small, whose operation or change of ownership escaped the notice of the press, though the making of coarse cloth to employ the prisoners in Bodmin gaol was noted. Wool from sheep grazed on Phillack and Gwithian towans, renowned for its fine quality, rated its own special annual fair, and the county was certainly self-sufficient in the wool trade.

It is noticeable that references to the industry are almost entirely confined to the first half of the century, implying a growing import of cloth, and although spinning and knitting were universal home employments, and often reached a high degree of skill, they leave behind traditional rather than tangible facts, if any, and spinning at home was an increasing rarity.

The fishing industry created a number of subsidiary trades: rope, net, cask, box, basket and crab-pot making, iron and copper smiths and foundrymen, timber merchants and their seasoning ponds, and chandlers. The larger ports had their own ropewalks through much of the nineteenth century, few traces now remaining except perhaps in a name. An instance lies in Falmouth where the long tarred shed stretching the length of the inland side of Dracaena Avenue until the late 1930s is now a street of long-established homes.

In every port, however small, nets were hand-made and mended with imported yarn and 'barked' in vats near the harbour to darken and preserve them. Machine manufacture was added in the nineteenth century in the busier ports and continued into the twentieth century, for instance the England family workshop in St Ives. The smaller makers were eventually out-priced by larger out-of-county specialists such as those of Bridport in Dorset.

Even in the eighteenth century and earlier, timber, such as Norway pine for masts and yards and tropical American and West Indian mahogany for interior furnishing, was imported to add to English – and Cornish – oak or elm. The importance of the timberyard is obvious, for harbour works, ship building and repair, and a vast range of other needs, but many are now turned to other uses with the seasoning ponds filled in and forgotten. The smallest of harbours saw boat building on the open beach or slipways as well as covered workshops through much of the century. The shipwrights, though often unlettered, were craftsmen of a high degree of skill, like James Goss of Calstock who would draw the lines of one of his fine vessels with his thumbnail on a plank and build with no further guide but his instinct, or Tommy Thomas of St Ives who would settle the ideal line for planking a boat with one sweep of his adze.

The extent of the cooperage trade may be judged from the pilchard export, which between 1800 and 1877 varied between 500 and 42,000 barrels a year, averaging 15,000 yearly. Added to that were the casks used in the early days of china clay export, plus those used for beer, apples and ships' stores. Now it is difficult to point with any certainty to the workplaces of that busy trade. The companion trade of basket making was also to be found in every port, but like the similar craft of making crab pots was frequently a backyard occupation.

The engineering side of mining has been touched on above, but many other trades contributed also. Tanners, cordwainers (shoemakers) and cobblers for industrial and personal leather goods, candlemakers and gunpowder manufacturers, potters and carpenters, smiths and masons, all could be found not far off in the workshops and markets of the Duchy. The Manor Tannery survives at Grampound, the last in this area and one of the few working traditionally, nationally, now making special leathers for Rolls Royce. Parish registers in mining areas, such as Zennor, show surprisingly large numbers of cordwainers in the nineteenth century. Local potteries, such as Lake's of Truro which worked well into the twentieth century, using clays from St Agnes Beacon, St Erth and some other sources with lead, tin and salt glazes, provided for the counthouse, inn and home. The city had many other trades befitting its importance: carpet making, woollen and knitting mills as well as the grist, paper-making, cart and wheel-wrights, tin and black-smiths, and all that goes with a busy market and social centre of a thriving community.

The great Cornishman Humphry Davy's miners' lamp was

Hawke's Cooperage at Truro, 1903–1918

designed for coal mining, and with no danger from gas the tin
miner worked by the light of tallow candles, each taking up to a
dozen with him to every core (shift). Candles were used with
maximum economy; for instance, climbing up at the end of a
core one man in two or three only carrying a light, but they
were also used to barter for tobacco or groceries. Underground,
the miner's vision was restricted to the few feet of candlelight
around him in otherwise impenetrable darkness, hard to imagine
in our electric world. *The Mining Journal* reported in 1864 that the
weekly consumption in Cornwall was 8,000 dozen at 5s. (25p)
for 12 lb ($5\frac{1}{4}$ kg), much of the tallow being imported. The chief
candlemakers were in Penzance, Penryn, Redruth, Truro and
Liskeard, with the enterprising Bolitho's of Penzance the chief
tallow merchants for this essential trade. The tallow candle
added considerably to the foul air of the mines with its smell and
sooty flame, but better refining of the tallow improved both the
light and the atmosphere as the century wore on. Better methods
of lighting the working area were used towards the end of the
century, such as acetylene, but not electricity.

Blasting is reputed to have been introduced to Cornwall by a
German, Becker, in a mine at St Agnes not long after 1670, and
it continued until after the invention of dynamite in 1867. The
use of 'black powder' with blasting carried out during cores,
plus the difficulty in many mines of giving effective ventilation,
created a foul atmosphere of fumes and dirty smoke in which it
was often difficult to see more than a few feet. Added to the
laborious work, wet conditions and the long climbs in the shaft
it helped substantially to shorten miners' lives.

Manufacture of black powder, and later other explosives, was
for obvious safety reasons carried out in remote and often
wooded spots. The largest works were in the Kennal Vale,
Ponsanooth; others were at Trago Mills and Herodsfoot near
Liskeard, Cosawes near Devoran, Garras, north of Idless near

Truro, Perranporth, Nancekuke north of Illogan and Hayle Towans. With the demand for military explosives several of these sites, Hayle for instance, producing 1,000 tons of cordite a year, only ceased work at the end of the 1914-18 war. Herodsfoot and Trago Mills served the Navy until 1965. Fuses for powder blasting were made of goose quills filled with black powder and were notoriously unreliable and the cause of many accidents. Several designs of safety fuse were made in the nineteenth century, mainly in the Camborne-Redruth area, the most effective by the Bickford Smith Co. in 1831 whose factory at Tuckingmill continued production well into this century.

Although Carlyle Spedding had lit his office with methane piped from his gassy Whitehaven mine in the 1740s, and some others experimented with the idea of coal gas lighting inconclusively, that illumination for factory, town and home was the invention of Boulton's Cornish agent William Murdoch. He had experimented with the properties of coal and in 1792 he 'cooked' coal in a closed vessel and piped gas to jets around his home in Cross Street, Redruth, for a light superior to candles or oil. In 1802 he fitted plant to gas-light part of Boulton's Soho Foundry in Birmingham, and the whole works the following year with improved 'batswing' jets.

Tregonning Hooper has suggested that Fox's Perran foundry had gas lighting in about 1799, which was soon extended to the whole village. Falmouth in 1819 was the first town to have gas light, first in the Royal Hotel in the heart of the town and later to nearby streets. Truro and Helston followed in 1822, Redruth in 1827, Penzance in 1830, Camborne and Launceston in 1834, St Ives in 1835, St Austell in 1836, Liskeard in 1839 and Wadebridge in the 1840s – perhaps an indicator of local prosperity. For all these works there were the nearby foundries to produce the retorts, piping, lamp standards and gas fittings at minimum transport costs. By the end of the century every

Cornish town of any size was served with gas, sometimes promoted by a nearby foundry for good business reasons.

Electric lighting for public or domestic use was only a feature of the twentieth century with two exceptions; a generating plant was built in St Austell in 1887, prompted by the use of private supplies by some of the china-clay workings, and, surprisingly, by a public supply in the village of Mevagissey. It was used at the Lizard Lighthouse as early as 1878, for a Redruth rugby match in 1879, and in a Redruth draper's in 1892. In the countryside at large, and for the less well-off candles and oil lamps were commonplace well into the twentieth century. The author remembers the flickering 25-cycle electric light replacing gas in the 1930s in a suburb of Falmouth.

The tall stacks needed for boiler houses, smelters, calciners, clay drys and kilns were built of granite up to the height above which the flue would have been too constricted by stone masonry so were completed further in brick. All brick was expensive to import and the county was served by its own brick kilns from quite early in the nineteenth century, about forty making fire, building and glazed items. Probably the best known of these works is that at Carbis, near Roche, where beehive kilns were used to fire building and fire bricks until 1940. The St Day Fire Brick and Clay Co., near Scorrier, was a major producer of a wide range of fire, facing, building and paving bricks, using iron-stained china clay, operating from 1860 to 1912. Although stone or cob were the common house-building materials for smaller homes some of the more imposing county houses are basically of brick faced with stone. Antony House near Torpoint, built 1718-29, is an example. In the nineteenth century brick or stone faced with stucco is commonplace, frequently only on the frontage. Industrial building sometimes used brick for details such as windows, until concrete became cheaper late in the century.

Lime for mortar was made at many ports in the county, imported limestone being burnt in substantial kilns on the quayside both for building and agriculture, as noted on p. 10.

Eighteenth century Cornwall, notwithstanding its maritime connections, was largely self-sufficient, even in the precision crafts of instrument and clock-making. Most of the major towns had makers of longcase and wall clocks, and 150 local craftsmen have been noted, for instance John Belling (1823) of Bodmin, one of a long line of clockmakers going back to 1685, who used tin to trim the spandrels (corner decorations) of his clock faces. His descendants in this century have changed to making electric cookers, a major industry until its closure in the slump of 1992. The makers' market was limited to the better-off middle class and the wealthy. Occasionally these local clocks can still be seen

The lime kiln, Harvey's Dock, Hayle

in antique sales, and more rarely 'dials' for mine surveying, such as the fine pieces by William Wilton (1801-1860) of St Day.

As travel became easier in the early nineteenth century imports from specialists in Birmingham and America brought the craft to an end, though town and village 'clockmakers' were fitting bought-in movements to locally painted dials for the cheaper mass market. In 1831, eighty-three watch and clock makers were recorded in Cornwall, but only a few could have been the creators of the movements they were using.

All these exhausting manual occupations required refreshment from the traditional British brew: small beer in the home until religion and cheap tea supplanted it, and strong ale for the working man from a host of outlets. From the cottage brew of the kiddlywink (beer shop), the home brew of many inns, to the large town breweries supplying homes and inns in their environs, the Duchy was well served. St Ives, for instance, in the 1830s had at least eighteen inns as well as a number of spirit shops (often supplied with contraband up to the 1870s) and kiddlywinks. The larger breweries were not all long-lived but the main towns always had a supplier. In 1873 there were one or more company breweries in Penzance, Helston, Redruth, Falmouth, St Agnes, Truro, Bodmin and Saltash. Their number was already shrinking by the end of the century, and the twentieth saw them dwindle to two. How many inns brewed their own must have fluctuated greatly but the several that survived well into the twentieth century shows the strength of the tradition of local brewing. Only the Blue Anchor in Helston continues independent brewing today. Some traces of local breweries, the conical ventilators usually, could be seen until recently, for instance, on the A39 near Penryn, and on the quay at Tresillian, near Truro.

CHAPTER 12

Privilege and Underprivilege

His fourscore years have bent a back of oak,
His earth-brown cheeks are full of hollow pits,
His gnarled hands wander idly as he sits
Bending above the hearthstone's feeble smoke.
Threescore and ten slow years he tilled the land;
He wrung his bread out of the stubborn soil;
He saw his masters flourish through his toil;
He held their substance in his horny hand.

Now he is old: he asks for daily bread;
He who has sowed the bread he may not taste
Begs for the crumbs: he would do no man wrong.
The Parish Guardians, when his case is read,
Will grant him, yet with no unseemly haste,
Just seventeen pence to starve on, seven days long.

Poems, Arthur Symons, 1865-1945

ONE striking feature of the landed gentry homes in Cornwall is their close association with the source of their wealth. In contrast with so many great English houses where the farm complex and stabling is discreetly removed to a distance, or behind a screen of trees, the rear entrance of the Cornish manor more often than not opens onto the farmyard and its suite of buildings. Some examples are Pendeen, Trewinnard, Godolphin, Trewithen, Trerice, Roscarrock, Cotehele and Antony. It may be that this closeness of master and man was the essential strength of the citizen Cornish Army in the Civil War.

The losses in that war were so great that the life of the county did not recover for a century, and then it was by way of the

growing mining industry and a new wealthy middle class profit-
ing from below, and not on, the land. The landowners also
benefited greatly from what lay beneath their estates by rents and
dues, the outstanding example being the Dukes of Bedford on
the Cornwall-Devon border, but it was wealth which divorced
them from their tenantry, and often from the county.

The miners' lives were extremely harsh, too often cut short by
accident or illness, but there was always the lure of a 'sturt', a
lucky strike on rich ground which might take the tributer
towards money he could invest, and perhaps on into a more
leisured class. Such good fortune was rare, and for the ordinary
miner, as for the farm worker and fisherman, infirmity or old age
could mean a bleak and lonely end in a workhouse ward,
separated from his wife, family and the community in which he
had lived, or the indignity of grudging charity at home.

The Poor

UP to the 1830s the Elizabethan Poor Law, with some amend-
ments, was the effective guardian of the poverty stricken.
Established parishioners could appeal to the Overseers of the
Poor to receive outdoor relief, which would be granted on a
scale established locally and varied with the price of bread
modified by the prosperity of the parish and the character of the
overseers. For newcomers to a parish the poor had little recourse
but begging, and to many miners this came particularly hard
for new mines were often in poor moorland parishes where a
successful venture could bring a flood of workers, turning hamlets into towns. Slightly better conditions might be found in
some of the older towns where charity or the parish had built or
rented almshouses and a couple could at least remain together
in old age, but consideration or generosity were rarely the

motivation of the overseers. The poorhouses and almshouses largely disappeared or were re-used as old people's homes after the passing of the Poor Law Amendment Act of 1834, but a fine example still stands near St Germans. Even a busy town like St Ives had no regular poorhouse but farmed its paupers out with 1s. to 3s. (5-15p) subsistence. The average round the county was a weekly 2s.(10p).

Homes and Houses

THE miners' lot was not improved by the common practice of houses being leased on 'three lives', which obtained until late in the nineteenth century, an instance being the sale of houses on the Trevethoe, Lelant, estate in 1926, when two properties were still held, one on three and one on two lives, the oldest being sixty-eight and the youngest fifty-four. (Trevethoe was one home of the Praed banking family of Truro, William being the financier for the Grand Junction Canal opened in 1805). Cottages or land, often profitless waste or heath, were leased at nominal rents with the proviso that when the last of three named persons died the property with all its buildings and improvements reverted to the landlord, who might renew the lease after imposing a 'fine' or keep it for his own purposes. With the health standards of those times such a lease was an obvious gamble; three healthy youngsters might succumb in a local epidemic, and years of hard labour become a gift to the landlord. Yet, such was the desire of Cornishmen for homes with a plot of land that thousands of acres of wasteland were patiently cleared and brought into cultivation for the ultimate benefit of landowners who might otherwise never have undertaken the work.

One staggering example is that of William Pearce of Landewednack, fifty years old, without the use of one arm, and with a wife and seven children to support. Over the course of eighteen years he worked five days a week delivering coal and other jobs with his mare and cart to earn the shilling (5p) a day on which he kept his family. He leased fourteen acres of bleak Lizard heath from Sir C. Hawkins, and in his spare time cleared the underlying rocks and boulders, created a tilth with sand and seaweed hauled from the shore two miles away, hedged, ditched and drained the plot into eight fields, and built a turf and thatch house with a stable, barn, cartshed and outhouses for three horses, one cow and five young cattle. Finally, in 1803, he reaped ten bushels of barley, ten of corn, two hogsheads of oats and nine trusses of hay. His reward was a silver medal and fifteen guineas (£15.75p) and the land for his children for the lifetime of the oldest of three named people. Such single-minded determination seems quite beyond comment. This was an extreme case, but the short-term security of such leases was the ambition of very many of the working poor.

An even stranger form of legal ownership was the 'one night house'. Failing any other place to go, a young couple would find a piece of waste ground, often on a wayside, and secretly gather cob, thatch, timber, door and window. When all the necessary material was collected they would muster their friends, and between dusk and dawn throw up four walls, roof them and set in the door and window. Once this primitive shack was occupied the couple could improve the building and its comforts, and perhaps expand. The cob walls well limewashed, and tarred for a few feet from the ground, could be long lived, but once unroofed and abandoned seem to melt away with hardly a trace. Narrow plots between country roads and farm fields can still be seen quite commonly and must mark some lost one-night homes.

The old Poor Law was inequitable and very varied in its application, and an enquiry started in 1832 led to the Poor Law Amendment Act of 1834, which was to become the most hated piece of legislation of the century. It was intended to standardise the treatment of the poor throughout the country, doing away with all outdoor relief, except for the infirm and some aged. All applicants were to be taken into workhouses, segregated by sex, and given some form of occupation to help with their keep. Parishes were to group together to fund the building of a Union Workhouse, the general plan being an entrance block which housed the management, and behind it two exercise yards separated by a high wall backed by multi-storeyed blocks of long wards heated by one or two small hearths. A small infirmary was also added. No provision was made for married couples, but mothers with young children were not separated from them until the boys were ten, or often younger. Conditions and discipline were of a kind to discourage all but the desperate from seeking admission.

Though the terms of some bequests kept their almshouses in service the new Act closed the parish poorhouses for good. Of many there was little to commend, but they varied in their management and seem rarely to have aroused the hatred and fear felt for their successors. In the eighteenth century many were ordinary houses; for instance Redruth had three adjoining two-storey houses in the town, and the hamlet of Zennor, with many mines in the parish, had a purpose-built two-storey house above Higher Tregerthen a mile away from the churchtown.

To implement the Act Cornwall was divided into thirteen parish groups, and by mid-June 1837 all had new buildings under way. Boards of Guardians for each Union were elected, seeming almost without exception to be of the professional classes. Each parish paid for the running costs in proportion to the number of its paupers in the Union, imposing hardship on the poorer parishes, but after 1866 the costs were met by a common fund. Inevitably expenses were kept to a minimum, as may be judged by the dietary of Madron (the Penwith area) Workhouse in 1842, slightly reduced from the supply initially

Madron Workhouse in disuse

Ward interior at Madron Workhouse

given. Breakfast and supper were the same; seven ounces of bread for men and women with $1\frac{1}{2}$ pints of tea for men and 1 pint for women, apparently without milk. Dinner was 5 oz of cooked meat and vegetable on Sunday, Wednesday and Friday; on Tuesday, Thursday and Saturday the meal was 4 oz. of fish; each day except Monday all dinners had $1\frac{1}{4}$lb of potatoes as well, for both sexes. To offset this indulgent living the Monday dinner was 4 oz of bread with $1\frac{1}{2}$ pints of vegetable soup for men, and 1 pint for women. The bread was usually made of equal parts of seconds wheat and barley, but sometimes of barley only if wheat was short and costly. That workhouse was notorious for its 'economical' relief. Little wonder that the Union Workhouses soon became re-christened 'Bastilles'.

In the second half of the century, as mining began to contract, emigration of miners to new mining fields abroad created a new class of paupers: wives and children left to fend for themselves until their men could send money home. Such families looked to relatives and friends for help rather than face the indignities offered by the Poor Law, and the probability that the woman would not be given outdoor relief for twelve months and, if there were several children, the certainty that some would be taken to the Union until they were nine years old and could be 'apprenticed'. The attitude which equated poverty with crime, and termed it self-inflicted through failure to make savings, persisted to the end of the century and into the twentieth. It was particularly unfeeling when the second half of the nineteenth century saw increasing unemployment, reduction in wages and a rising cost of bread.

Punishment

WITH such consideration given to the hapless poor, the fate of the apprehended sinner was even less likely to be sympathetic.

One example may be taken from the sentences passed at the
County Assizes of August 1813; taking the identifying thread
from naval cordage, 14 years transportation; a woman who set
fire to a mow (a small stack of shocks) of corn, hanging; stealing
and killing a sheep, death; housebreaking and robbery, death,
but it must be noted that most courts were hesitant in pressing
for the death sentence, and imposed a lesser penalty. In 1815
theft of three pounds of candles (worth about 6p) was punished
by a month in jail and public whipping. As late as 1843 a twelve
year old boy, for stealing some currant cakes, raisins and wal-
nuts, was sentenced to seven years transportation, and his ten
year old accomplice a few days imprisonment and whipping.
Most towns had stocks which were used for petty mis-
demeanours such as drunkenness; the normal stay was for six
hours, and the last recorded use was in Camborne as late as 1866.

The boroughs had cells ('clinks') for short-term imprisonment, but must have been a severe punishment in themselves.
Camborne clink was said to be 6 feet (1m 83 cm) long by 5½ feet
(1m 67.5 cm) wide and six feet high, St Ives was much the same,
and Truro's was strewn with straw, with a block in the centre to
which the prisoner was chained, unventilated and with no privy.
Launceston town jail was described in 1812 as 'in a most filthy
and delapidated state', with no water, privy or exercise space,
and with some room doors only 4 feet high (1m 22cm) and
15 inches (38 cm) wide, other rooms having windows 3 feet
(91.5cm) high and 9 inches (23 cm) wide with an iron bar set
in. Despite these horrors the newspapers through the century
are filled with reports of murder, violence, robbery, riot and
drunkenness no less than our own today.

In 1871 the *West Briton* reported that the County jail at
Bodmin, whose grim remains still stand, could hold 141 males,
59 females and 25 debtors, with a daily average of 102.
Hard labour, first class, consisted of rope-beating (softening

tar-hardened rope) and the treadmill, on which 32 men worked for four hours, alternating with a second 32 'resting' by picking oakum: unravelling old tarred ships' rigging to be used for caulking ships' decks. Penzance had a treadmill also. Second class hard labour was oakum picking, mat making and other trades. For the women needlework, knitting, washing clothes and oakum picking kept them employed. Their diet, probably not unlike that noted at Madron Workhouse, was described as 'punitive' though not so as to endanger the health and strength of the prisoners, with debtors getting the same with extra bread. However, a visitor to the Stannary Jail at Lostwithiel noted a debtor who was allowed access to a grated window where he could beg with a shoe hung from a cord to avoid him starving, but that was in 1805. There seems no great difference between workhouse and prison save that the felons had a given time to serve, and a hope of freedom to come. For the poor, whether driven to the workhouse or to crime, their poverty was regarded not as a product of their times but as the avoidable error of their ways, with little distinction between great and petty crime. Some of their betters might make distinction between deserving and undeserving poor, but the law and many of the better off, too, rarely did.

Child labour was the standard for much of the century, though women and girls were not permitted below ground in Cornish mines, only being employed in surface work, 'spalling' (breaking and sorting ore) or at the washing processes for at least 4d. to 6d. ($1\frac{1}{2}$p to $2\frac{1}{2}$p) a ton, or at best 1s. to 1s.6d.(5p to 6p) per day. In St Just in 1842 girl spallers were earning 8d. to 9d. ($3\frac{1}{2}$ to 4p) a day. Rarely, boys as young as 7 or 8 worked underground, probably with a close relative, and in Cornwall and west Devon a report by Dr Charles Barham in 1842 estimated that nine to ten thousand youngsters were employed at the mines, three thousand being under 13. At least 424 boys

under 15 were working underground, including night work, for
shifts of 6 to 8 hours according to the hardness of their work.
And after the working shift there were several hundreds of feet
of ladders to climb back up to grass. George Henwood, writing
in the *Mining Journal* between 1857 and 1859 noted several
instances of boys between 7 and 10 working below ground and
he commented 'this is the fate of hundreds of children no more
than eight years of age!' Usually boys were sorting ores or
working in the wet slime of the buddles (washing tables) up to
14 years, before going underground.

Wages could start at 2s. (10p) per month for the youngest and
rise to 16s. (80p) for a fifteen year old, with, of course, no
account taken of the miles that might have to be walked to and
from the 'bal' (mine), or of the time taken climbing down and
up the shaft. To work the morning shift could mean rising at
4 a.m., and the afternoon shift often meant reaching home and
bed as late as 10 p.m. If ore sampling was about to take place the
children could work both shifts from 6 a.m. to 8 p.m., with no
more than half an hour for dinner. George Henwood remarks:
'Solitary confinement and hard labour for eight hours are
deemed punishment for criminals; what was this?'

Recommendations were made setting a minimum age for
underground work, and the number of hours to be worked for
various age groups, but little attention was paid to them before
the 1878 Factories Act extended its control to all industries. The
fate of children of fishermen and farm workers was perhaps less
hard. For the seamen's sons the skills of the calling were learnt
at an early age though young boys were not employable at sea.
In season they could give some help with the landed catches, but
with pilchards most of the shore work fell on the women. For
the farming child the worst would be stone clearing in the fields,
barefoot on a cold winter's day, and there are many surviving
accounts of that misery. At least the summers might offer some

compensation, unlike the eternal dark of the mines. For the very young and for girls straw plaiting was one possible task, but the skills of spinning and knitting only came with experience. There were endless tasks on the farm, water carrying, stock feeding and minding, weeding, bird-scaring and so on, to keep all members of the family save the babies busy, too often with little or no payment.

Education

WITH child labour, however ill-paid, an essential extra to the family income of many poor households, education had a very low priority indeed, and was not encouraged by the contempt of many of the traditional mine captains for book learning. Only the county gentry educated their children as a matter of course, with tutors for the boys, followed by public school and Oxford, or more rarely Cambridge, before returning to their estates, the Anglican church or the armed services. Public Schools and Universities alike offered little more than Latin and Greek, with teaching and examination standards probably at the lowest level in their history. Only in some of the Dissenters' academies was practical education offered, and it was not until Butler at Shrewsbury and Arnold at Rugby brought wider syllabuses into being that the Public Schools began to face the real world. For the girls a governess to instruct in ladylike accomplishments was considered sufficient. The lesser gentry sent their sons to a nearby Grammar School, and though every town of any size in the county had its school, the fees and the standard of teaching varied greatly, often going no further than the three Rs with some Latin and Greek.

Truro had such a school, founded in 1549 in St Mary's Street, offering Latin until the Principal, Cornelius Cardew, retired in

1805, when Thomas Hogg introduced more liberal studies. He published a book on mineralogy in 1825 drawing considerably from Cornish materials. Penryn, a borough since 1236, had a Grammar School attached to the Collegiate Church as early as 1247, and also a similar monastic foundation, but these were abolished and replaced by an Edward VI Grammar or 'Latin' school which survived to the nineteenth century, replaced by a National School. Saltash, St Mary Week and Bodmin also had Grammar Schools of Edward VI foundation, variously surviving, as did Fowey from 1692, founded by its Corporation. When that school was re-housed in 1880 navigation was added to the syllabus, and a girls' school was opened in the late 1850s.

In East Looe a Mathematical School was opened in 1716, funded by a legacy, and operated into the nineteenth century with navigation as one of its subjects. Early in the eighteenth century 'Blue Boys' schools were founded by and at the charge

Truro School interior

of John Buller of Shillingham at Grampound, Liskeard, Looe, Penryn and Saltash, the best pupil in each to be apprenticed to a trade. Helston School headmaster in the 1830s and until 1842 was Derwent Coleridge, son of the poet Samuel Taylor Coleridge, but heads and staff were usually churchmen.

Falmouth had a charity school for sixty poor children opened in 1802, and a similar girls' Free School opened in 1811, to be increased by Lancastrian and National Schools in 1812 and 1827. The élite school of the town was the Classical and Mathematical School opened in 1825 with five university-educated staff in a fine building halfway up Killigrew Street. After 1855 it was reorganised and renamed the Grammar School, remaining in the same building until 1914.

Some children of the poor went to Dame Schools, often run by women offering little more than child-minding, while the better ones would teach the three Rs, within their own limitations, for a weekly fee of 1d. or 2d. (less than 1p), sometimes paid in kind with produce or candles. In 1840 there were about 120 Dame Schools in the county. A few of the larger mines had primary schools, with an obvious bias towards mining needs, but what learning there was, reinforced by a 'custis' (a slat of wood) and the dunce's cap, usually ended at ten when the children went to work at the mines. Farming children too often did not even have that chance to learn those limited rudiments. Sunday schools, Nonconformist or Church of England, had a different purpose, but also gave some children their introduction to reading and writing.

In 1835 a private school, Trevarth House, was started by mine agents in Gwennap 'to enable their children to acquire the rudiments of such scientific knowledge as bore on mining operations' – a remarkable piece of enlightened self-interest for its time, as was a similar school started a little later in Camborne. By 1842 Trevarth school had 52 pupils, only a small fraction of the children of the parish. At the same date a Report on the State of Education in the Mining Districts of Cornwall by Seymour Tremenheere noted 38 'Common Day Schools for the Elementary Education of the working classes' in seven mining parishes from Tywardreath to St Just, but teaching only 1,614 children from a total population of 51,500.

In October 1838 Sir Charles Lemon offered to endow a mining school in Truro, but only 14 pupils were taught between 1839 and 1840. Later in 1840 Sir Charles offered £20,000 towards a mining college if the larger mines would provide a levy from their profits to sustain it – a sum of about £1,500 – but the mine adventurers declined and the offer was withdrawn. Cornwall was without a mining school, except for some 'travelling schools', until 1896, when the Camborne School of Mines absorbed the scattered part-time schools of Camborne, Penzance, Redruth and Truro.

An interesting insight into education in a Cornish town quoted below is given in the reminiscences of William Paynter of St Ives recorded by his daughter in 1927, but reaching back some ninety years. The grammar school described about the 1840s was proposed by the Borough Charter of 1639, and was to have a master and usher, with the Bishop of Exeter, the Mayor and Aldermen as Governors. It was opened in 1649 with a grant of £3 10s., and the master, who was usually Town Clerk also, had an annual salary of £5, rising to £10 in the late seventeenth century. Apart from Dame schools in the 1820s there were schools run by the Wesleyan Chapel until 1870, and in 1822 a Free School was opened by Sir Christopher Hawkins, a con-siderable beneficiary to the town, for the education of poor children. It was in Shute Street, now Street-an-Pol, and com-monly called the Navigation School, as that was taught to boys at a charge of 1d. per week. The Grammar School or 'Academy' was at the top of a long flight of steps still carrying that name,and was attended by both boys and girls. Even in winter school started at 7 a.m., before a fire was lit, and the pupils each provided their own tallow candle, the only light and heat until they were released for breakfast. Morning and afternoon school followed though Paynter does not specify the hours. Teaching was based heavily on books of questions and answers with little or no information to expand the bare facts of the answers, only to be learnt by heart without thought. The same books were used for homework, taken in the same classroom, to learn answers to be tested the next day. The teacher was assisted by an usher who taught the youngest and learnt what he could himself, a pupil-teacher in effect. A great deal of time was given to penmanship and drawing, and Paynter found geography was, for him, the best taught subject, places were pointed out and named on wall-maps, and much time was spent on drawing maps and learning the 'use of the globes'. His own proudest achievement was a large genealogical chart of the kings and queens of England.

Illiteracy remained widespread, until W. E. Forster's Education Act of 1870 brought about the establishment of locally elected School Boards which were to be funded from Government grants and local rates to provide schools for five to ten-year-old children, wherever Nonconformist British, or C. of E. National, schools were not already opened. When the Board Schools were built, St Austell the first in 1872 at a cost of £945 for 375 pupils, and St Ives in 1880, there was elementary education for all, except for those who chose to minch, and they had to face the 'whipper-in'.

It was in the remote Isles of Scilly that education for all children was first introduced. The Godolphins and the Society for the Propagation of Christian Knowledge had built schools in the islands, but Augustus Smith built new premises, and decreed compulsory attendance in 1850, thirty years before the Forster Act in England. He charged a penny a week for instruction, or two pence for 'minchers', making sure of attendance. Educated islanders were recruited as teachers and Smith himself taught navigation.

Lack of education was not so much a matter of choice as of economic pressure, and in later life, as established family men, the keener miners supported their own educational centres, for instance St Just Miners' Institute, Carharrack Institution, St Agnes Miners' and Mechanics' Institute, Tywardreath Useful Knowledge Society and Roche Farmers', Mechanics' and Miners' Institute. To such venues the leading geologists, mining and steam engineers were invited to speak, and found audiences with such intelligent appreciation as to make their long journeys well worth while. Apart from these local associations the prestigious Royal Institution of Cornwall in Truro, the Royal Cornwall Polytechnic Society in Falmouth, and the Royal Geological Society of Cornwall in Penzance, though promoted and patronised by the educated middle classes, the Polytechnic, for instance, by Anna Maria Fox and her brother and sister, played an important part in the education of the county's workers.

Health and Hospitals

THE mine surgeon has already been mentioned briefly, the only help for the injured miner, which was only given at the surface, for the doctor never went underground. The only place for the injured man to be taken was his own home, always small and probably overcrowded with children, for the miner usually married very young. There were homes where the stairs were too narrow for the man to be taken up to his bed so that he had to lie amid the bustle of the kitchen-living room, and it was not unknown for the patient to share the only bed with wife and children.

The mine club paid 1s. (5p) a day or 30s. (£1.50) a month for injury, and some clubs might pay for attendance, bandaging or bedding if required, but for the miner broken by age or the dreaded phthisis (a progressive wasting disease of the lungs caused by rock dust) no help was given. If a miner died of injury the club provided the burial, or if of other causes, paid for the coffin. His widow was generally allowed £10, but if the mine closed all these benefits ended. At the four mines of Joseph Thomas Austin's (later Treffry) Fowey Consolidated Copper each miner was paid thirty shillings (£1.50) a month while ill, with doctor and medicine for his family as well. This was funded by a stoppage of 1s.9d. (app.9p) from each miner's monthly earnings – probably better than in most Cornish mines.

In the 1790s Sir Francis Basset, Sir John St Aubyn and Sir William Lemon moved the building of a public hospital, and land was bought on the hillside south of City Road, Truro, for £206. The foundation stone of the building, which was to cost no more than £2,000, was laid on August 13th, 1792, and the Cornwall General Infirmary opened on August 12th, 1799, with beds for 20 patients, women on the first floor and men on the second, cared for by a matron and three to six nurses. Miners were rarely accepted and often there were as many as eight beds unoccupied. In 1842 a Public Dispensary opened in the city which for long treated more patients than the hospital. Later elevated to the title of Royal Cornwall Infirmary, it saw slow and steady expansion, particularly in the twentieth century, to its present unwieldy conglomeration. It will be closed in the 1990s, with its services moved to Treliske, and the old site turned to other use.

A Public Dispensary was opened in Falmouth in 1806, adding to various charities, but, apart from the service of several doctors, the town had to wait for the Cottage Hospital and Nursing Home until 1883, and the present hospital after 1893. There was, however, a Royal Cornwall Sailors' Home and Hospital opened in 1852, near the harbour, on the Bank at the end of Arwenack Street.

For long, and certainly by the 1840s, there was an obvious and urgent need for a miners' hospital, but when the matter was pressed both miners and management were reluctant or openly hostile. Bearing in mind the nature of transport and roads then, it is perhaps understandable in those who might face a long, agonising and perhaps fatal journey. Finally, in 1863, the West Cornwall Hospital for Convalescent Miners was opened on land given by R.T.C. Agar-Robartes of Lanhydrock on Blowinghouse Hill, Redruth. An accident ward was added in 1871 and a women's ward in 1890, with the name being changed in 1902 to the Camborne and Redruth Miners' and Women's Hospital, still serving the community.

An East Cornwall Hospital was established in Bodmin in 1844, surprisingly long after the Cornwall Mental Hospital (St Lawrence's) of 1820, outside the town. Another hospital for the east of the region was built in Launceston in 1862, and a Passmore Edwards cottage hospital at Liskeard in 1895/96. St Ives, despite its trading wealth, had no hospital until 1920, and Helston's, too came late.

The miners and the sick of West Cornwall were first served by the Penzance Public Dispensary and Humane Society, planned and directed by John Bingham Borlase, great-nephew of the antiquarian, and established in rooms above an old almshouse in Market Jew Street in 1809. This moved to Chapel Street in 1813 after Borlase's death, and to another house in the same street in 1823. Finally in 1874 a proper hospital was built on the edge of town in St Clare Street and the dispensary amalgamated with it, with a new wing subvented by the Bolitho family in 1887, and a further wing in 1896. Enlargements are still continuing.

CHAPTER 13

This World and the Next

Man without religion is the creature of circumstances.
A.W. Hare

POVERTY and the struggle for survival can drain the human spirit and destroy civilised society when – and wherever they are found in mankind's communities. For the working inhabitants of Cornwall, supported by an agriculture which in the main had fertile but few first-grade soils and a mild but wet and windy climate, and by a fishery rich in quantity but far from good markets, plus a mineral industry which, whether surface or underground, was hedged about with restrictions, taxes and poor pay, life was hard and rarely rewarding. When chance offered a prize out of the blue, such as a wreck, the normal standards of neighbourliness and even humanity could too easily be forgotten by people who normally were as honourable as any in the nation. Up to the eighteenth century at least it was the lords of the coastal manors who squabbled over the profits of misfortune as much as the common people, and such prize-taking was certainly not limited to Cornwall. Too much has been made of the 'wreckers'. The hard life of the miner, often near absolute poverty from the vagaries endemic to the industry, was undoubtedly the cause of some savage and violent wrecking incidents but they were few and grew less to none in the nineteenth century. It must also not be forgotten that it was a Cornishman, Henry Trengrouse of Helston, who demonstrated the first means of saving crews of ships wrecked when no boat could approach, in June 1816. His rocket apparatus was only discarded in 1989, to much protest.

Even more must be recalled the selfless bravery of innumerable efforts by individuals, local gigs, pilot boats and fishing craft who risked all to save strangers facing disaster from storms on the dangerous Cornish coast. From the first special rescue boat, manned by coastguards, provided in St Ives in the late eighteenth century and the first Penzance lifeboat of 1824 inspired by the formation of the Royal National Institution for the Preservation of Life from Shipwreck (forerunner of the RNLI), twenty-two lifeboat stations were opened in the county funded by caring individuals and manned by volunteers. The service records of their lifeboats is a proud story of hundreds of lives saved, only too often in circumstances of extreme danger, and sometimes with the loss of the rescuers.

Another aspect of the misery of poverty was the solace of drunkenness to which men, women and even children were driven, with all the attendant squalor and suffering that can threaten. The heat and hard labour of mining added to its danger made drinking customary throughout the industry everywhere, with inevitably some falling into excess, wasting their income and crippling family life; not a new scenario nor one that has disappeared.

In such a society the guidance and help of religion could have been a mitigating influence, and in some few parishes there were pastors who gave example and aid, but they were indeed few. In the eighteenth century the Established Church had reached a very low level of its Christian duty. Throughout the country, and in Cornwall no less, more than half of parish livings were in the gift of the landed gentry, to be disposed at the whim of the proprietor like any other part of his property. The result was that some incumbents were younger sons, or 'the fool of the family' for whom there was no place on the family estates, or hunting cronies of the landlord, whose pretensions to religious dedication were minimal but who were adamant about the tithes and other income from their parish which gave them a comfortable stipend. A further dubious practice was that of plural livings, some clergy serving as many as four parishes, not necessarily adjacent. There were instances in Cornwall of vicars whose parishes were more than a day's journey apart, yet not always served by a curate in the absence of the incumbent. Delayed or neglected christenings, churchings and burials are on record, and erratic services or none compounded the general decay of pastoral care.

It is not surprising, therefore, that when two enthusiastic clergymen arrived in the county in 1743, preaching with fire and conviction, they were received with active, and sometimes violent, hostility by both clergy and laity. Charles came in July and John Wesley seven weeks later, the first of thirty-two visits he made to the Duchy. Though he was, and remained, an ordained Church of England minister, pulpits were usually denied him; his preaching was in the open from whatever vantage point he could find to raise him above the crowd, only occasionally in a meeting room. Threats, riot, abuse and violence marked many of his early meetings, but as time passed his congregations grew far beyond the capacity of any church to house, and his journeys through the county became much like a royal progress. His energy was astounding; in a region of poor roads and wide expanses of rough moorland he would ride great distances in all weathers to gathering after gathering of antagonistic as well as friendly crowds to give his witness. He records one three-day weekend when 6 sermons were preached in places scattered over 50 miles of rough riding, and another of 25 miles between 6 sermons in 30 hours, and this by a man who had commented on his weak constitution! Forty-six years after his first visit he could write: 'There is a fair prospect in Cornwall from Launceston to the Land's End,' and fair it was with a chapel in every town in the county and overflowing congregations, many of whom attended the usual church services in addition to their chapel worship. The revived faith radically changed the lifestyle of a large proportion of miners, some of whom became lay preachers of considerable impact, though largely unlettered and decidedly earthy.

During the next century wherever there was a body of people, whether of miners, farmers or fishers, chapels would spring up, often built by their congregation, and where, today, there sometimes seem few signs left of where the worshippers could have come from. A simple instance comes from the three and a half mile lane from Halsetown to Lelant beside which four chapels stood. A reason for so many places of worship was the intensity of feelings and beliefs of the converted, leading to secession of minority groups with differences of opinion on practice or interpretation. An excellent picture of this fragmentation in a Cornish town is given in Bernard Deacon's *Liskeard and its People in the 19th Century*.

An older sect setting high moral standards were the Quakers. Outstanding among them were the Fox families of Falmouth. Barred from local and national politics, they were successful businessmen and reasonable employers, rising to join the Duchy's wealthier middle classes. Their acumen in the mining field, as pilchard export merchants, timber importers, engineering foundry owners, and other trades serving the county's needs, brought them well-sited and skilfully planted estates. From their modest houses they played an important part in the intellectual and social life of Cornwall, particularly of the Falmouth area.

The dangers and difficulties of mining may have been reduced but little during the nineteenth century, but the miners' lives above ground were transformed to a new social standard, and the faith that brought about the change was taken with them as declining work at home drove them into new ventures round the world.

CHAPTER 14

Buildings and Boroughs

There are a great many odd styles of architecture about.

J. Ruskin

IN every town there are buildings of architectural merit surviving though the architect is not always known, and even with the great country houses the designer is not always traceable, as with Antony House. Where he is known the architect is rarely Cornish, for instance John Nash at Caerhayes Castle in 1808. Trengwainton, near Penzance, in contrast, was the work of Edmund Davy, grandfather of Sir Humphry. Much of the nineteenth century church restoration was also by outsiders, for instance E. Sedding at King Charles the Martyr in Falmouth and St Neot, but one widely criticised was James Piers St Aubyn of the family long settled in the county.

One interesting Cornish connection lies in the Manor House in Princes Street, Truro, the Bath stone used being given to his nephew Thomas Daniell by Ralph Allen (1694-1764) the Cornish founder of the postal service and creator of part of Bath. The same stone was used for the Assembly Rooms, the front of which alone survives, and the remarkable range of Georgian houses in Lemon Street. Truro also housed the offices of Sylvanus Trevail (1851-1903) who designed a large proportion of the new Board Schools called for by the Education Act of 1870, outstandingly that in St Ives, where the adaptability of the interior has made possible a new lease of life as a community medical centre.

But, as was emphasised in chapters 8 and 11, Cornwall is rich in every kind of first-class building material, and as wealth from a flourishing mining industry spread into the economy so both gentry and yeomen used their new prosperity to improve their domestic comfort. There had been a great rebuild in Tudor times but it no longer satisfied the needs of a new age when so many houses, great and small, had suffered the ravages of time and a change of fashion.

The Carew house at Antony was replaced in 1721 by a great new house in classical style faced with Pentewan stone but lined with brick for warmth and comfort, and with brick-built wings. Brick was used internally in several houses built by Thomas Edwards of London; Tehidy, north of Camborne; Carclew, between Truro and Falmouth, home of the entrepreneur Sir Charles Lemon (now destroyed by fire); and Pendarves, near Camborne, all about the mid-eighteenth century. Pencarrow, near Bodmin, the Molesworth home, about the same period, merely had a modern plastered façade added to an older building. St Aubyn's Clowance, south of Camborne, built early in the nineteenth century was plain and simple granite. Port Eliot, near St Germans, built by Sir John Soane between 1802 and 1806; Prideaux, for the Rashleighs, near Luxulyan, in 1808 and massive Tregothnan built by William Wilkins of London for Lord Falmouth in 1816-18 all continued to use granite but in Tudor style, while Trelissick, built in 1825 by P.F. Robinson for Thomas Daniell of Truro, had granite for a great classical six-column portico facing down the Fal to the sea.

Directly or indirectly these great houses were paid for by mining, smelting, banking or china clay, and with few exceptions were designed by architects from outside the county, as already noted. Less well known are those responsible for the smaller town houses, homes of merchants, traders, mine captains and the professional middle classes whose status and well-being also derived from the mineral trades, even if at several removes.

The neat, well-proportioned stucco houses in terraces and squares of Georgian Penzance; the shallow Italiante roofs of some larger houses in Camborne and Redruth; the chequerboard brick frontage of Grove Place in Falmouth; 'one of the most completely Georgian streets preserved anywhere', Lemon Street of 1794 in Truro; and the simple, sturdy Georgian granite houses of Lostwithiel are some examples of the new era of domestic comfort following the fashions of England, though the public front most often has a rear of cheaper slaty stone. A search in any Cornish town will soon show more examples of solid stone or slate-hung homes of this period, despite tremendous losses since 1945.

Voyagers to, or through, Cornwall were no longer faced with little choice but squalid inns and lodging houses as new, well appointed hotels were built to serve ever increasing numbers of travellers on business at home or abroad. The Royal Hotel of about 1830 in Falmouth; the White Hart, 1838, across the road from Harvey's Foundry in Hayle, and Webb's Hotel, 1833, in Liskeard, are fair examples of the new businessmen's accommodation. Towards the end of the century came even larger hotels for tourists, Trevail's Headland Hotel in Newquay for instance.

Perhaps nothing shows the change in Cornish life more than the civic buildings which improved so many Cornish towns in the nineteenth century, a remarkable list of landmarks so easily taken for granted. Penzance Market House with its great Ionic columns and dome by W. Harris of Bristol in 1836, and the 1830 eccentricity of the Egyptian House in Chapel Street; Helston's granite Market House of 1839; the Institute and Reading Room with clocktower of 1884 at Porthleven; Redruth Town Hall in 1828; Camborne Town Hall and the Literary Institute of 1829; the stucco Ionic pillared Customs House, *c*. 1785, in Falmouth, and the Classical and Mathematical School of 1824 on Killigrew

Street; Truro Town Hall in Italianate Renaissance style by Christopher Eales in 1846 and St Austell Town Hall in similar style two years earlier; Liskeard Market Hall of 1821 and Town Hall in 1859; Bodmin Cattle Market in 1826 but the granite Assize Court not until 1873 by Bush of Launceston; and Launceston's Pannier Market of 1840. Lostwithiel, strangely, had preceded all with its Guildhall built in 1740 and Grammar School in 1781. So many buildings of quality and cost funded largely from the public purse show the growth of civic pride after the doldrums and decay of the century after the Civil War.

The coming of the Wesleys, too, had its architectural impact, from the simple wayside meeting houses of cob and thatch to the dignified respect-ability of buildings like the Centenary Chapel in Camborne, the Wesleyan Chapel and Schools of St Ives, or the Baptist Chapel in Launceston. These places of worship, dotted about the countryside and villages or enhancing the growing towns, owe far less to wealth than they do to religious enthusiasm and active faith.

Nor were the farm workers forgotten entirely, for Worgan and other writers on agriculture offered plans of improved cottages and many were built on the larger estates. The five round thatched cottages in Veryan, built by Hugh Rowe of Lostwithiel, are an oddity of the early nineteenth century, but not the only cornerless labourers' homes. In the main, however, the farm labourer still lived in squalid conditions well into the twentieth century, and the housing of too many miners was cramped, damp, stone or cob hovels, perhaps self-built.

CHAPTER 15

The Cornishman Abroad

Emigration only solved or ameliorated individual problems; in many places it only aggravated the social distress . . . each [emigrant] leaving behind, on the average, a wife and three children to whom he sent meagre and irregular remittances.

Cornwall in the Age of the Industrial Revolution, John Rowe

THE graph on p. 89 shows very clearly that Cornish mining reached its maximum output in the 1850s, tin a few years later than copper. From that high point the production of both metals diminished rapidly, copper faster and more nearly to extinction than tin. The causes were many; fewer new finds of rich ores at home, large and opulent finds in other continents, and easily worked alluvials in S.E. Asia all played their part. The consequence was inevitable: a large, skilled workforce with an ever-decreasing home market for its skills in a world largely indifferent to the welfare of the unfortunate.

As new mining areas opened up along the peninsula and others declined there were considerable movements of population following employment. The hamlets of Camborne and Redruth drew from far afield to grow into towns as the country round them was burrowed for copper and tin from the mid-eighteenth century. A movement west into Penwith at the same time saw the population grow rapidly, partly naturally with security of employment and partly from immigration from eastern parishes.

The 'Cornish Copper Kingdom' had suffered and weathered the threat from the open-cast Parys Mine in Anglesea which

163

flooded the market in and after 1770, but not without considerable hardship and some mine closures. Later recovery saw copper mining flourishing in the 1820s, in the Camborne-Redruth area, Gwennap and many parishes further west. Foreign ores were being imported early on, from Cuba and Chile in particular, but too little to affect prices. Mining in Cornwall moved eastwards, to the St Austell area, St Cleer parish and Caradon in the late 1830s, and to Gunnislake and Tavistock (Devon Great Consols just over the border) in the 1850s. There was hardship in the areas left behind, and movement to new fields, for instance from Penwith parishes to St Cleer, and abroad to Michigan. A tradition of 'following the work' was well established in the miners' way of life.

There was a not inconsiderable emigration within Great Britain, to the coal fields of Wales, northern England and Scotland, the iron mines of Cumbria, lead mines of the Pennines, and even in Cornwall to the 'inferior' clay industry. John Rowe estimated that 'It may ... be assumed that from 2,500 to 3,000 men ... found temporary or permanent work in the china clay industry, but that was only about a quarter of the men that lost their livelihood through the catastrophic collapse of the copper mining industry of Cornwall. The majority of the others emigrated.' In Derbyshire Cornish involvement was brought about from 1823-1859 when the Cornishman John Taylor became permanent consultant to the Duke of Devonshire for his Grassington Moor interests. A succession of resident Cornish managers was employed by the Duke, and they in turn looked back home when skilled labour was needed for mining or engineering. Once their ability was known they were recruited further north in the Pennines and into Shropshire. Nellie Kirkham makes the point specifically that it was with the introduction of steam pumping that the Cornish arrived in Derbyshire, and the same appears to have been the case in Shropshire.

To the iron mines of Cumberland A. Harris mentions the coming of 'James Floyd and his partners from Cornwall', and that the directors looked to Cornwall for their supply of pumping engines. That was hardly surprising in 1866 for the declining copper industry offered many disused machines. Harris states that 'There is little doubt that Cornishmen formed a significant proportion of the underground force at the mines as early as 1866', and that ' . . . by the end of the nineteenth century about half the men were said to be of Cornish origin. Cornish families were sufficiently numerous in Millom to have their own Bible Christian minister by 1870.' The same applied to the little village of Roose where the 1881 census showed families from Breage, Crowan, Gwennap, Illogan, Liskeard and St Ive, and six other Cornish parishes.

Cornish miners were not always popular in the coalfields of South Wales and the north, with something of a reputation of being blacklegs, but many did settle, and from miners or pumpmen the mines of the Isle of Man and Ireland also profited from the know-how learnt deep under Cornwall. The legend that any deep hole in the ground, anywhere in the world, would have a Cousin Jack at the bottom of it was getting well established.

As at home, it was hard-rock mining prowess and steam pump proficiency that took Cornishmen abroad to find employment. One of the earliest was the man of many initiatives, Richard Trevithick. His adventures in South America between 1816 and 1827 are only of concern here in that mining in Peru, and more importantly in Chile, was brought to the attention of the engineers and foundrymen of Cornwall as a new market for the improving Cornish engines. Chile was later to become one of the agents in the downfall of copper mining in the South-west. Mexico, with its enviable output of silver, became a focus of mining attention at almost the same time. John Taylor, mentioned above, in 1819 recommended the former President of the

College of Mining in Mexico City to employ a Cornish miner, Robert Phillips, to bring out a steam engine to demonstrate its efficiency in mine drainage. Mines there were still being unwatered by men carrying buckets or by horse whims. A Scot, Capt. James Vetch, was finally brought out to organise, with John Rule, a mine captain from Camborne, as technical overseer. Rule recruited a large skilled team, many Cornish, to reorganise the Real del Monte mines totally, bringing them to partial success in the face of vast political, practical and climatic difficulties. By 1849, however, the concern was losing heavily and was sold to Mexican owners. Brazil, too, had its Cornish; Rowe notes that 'As early as 1870 there were not less than 85 Cornishmen at the Tocapilla mine . . . earning . . . a total wage thrice that which they had been able to secure even in "good times" in Cornwall.'

The British Government of the day could find no better use for the great Southern Continent than as a dump for convicts, in Tasmania in 1803 and 1804, and at Moreton Bay in southern Queensland a little later. Ill-organised settlements were made at the Swan River in Western Australia and in South Australia in 1836, but it was articles published between 1830 and 1833 by Edward Gibbon Wakefield promoting the idea of colonisation by business men, yeoman farmers and labourers that changed the face of immigration. A follower of his ideas, John Stephens, son of a miner-Methodist minister of Helston, published *The Land of Promise* in 1839, painting a rosy picture of settlement in South Australia.

By 1840, in applications for free passage to South Australia from 43 Cornish parishes, there were 10 from farmers, 12 from blacksmiths, 27 from agricultural labourers and 132 from miners out of a total of 245 in 25 occupations. The great invasion came with a 'copper rush' in 1847. In April that year 700 left Camborne for Australia and the United States. In 1849 a Truro

TO
MINERS,
Masons, Carpenters, and all per sons engaged in building, Blacksmiths,
AGRICULTURAL
LABORERS
And Mechanics generally.

Eligible married persons under 35 years of age, may have

AN EARLY FREE PASSAGE
TO
NEW
ZEALAND
ON APPLICATION
To Mr. LATIMER, Truro.

Married people above 40 years of age, may have a *free passage* if they have one child 14 years of age and upwards, for every year that the parents exceed 40,---that is, a father 42 years of age, or about, will be acceptable if he has 2 children above 14.

(c. 1840)

To Sail the First of April,

1841,

FOR QUEBEC,

The fine fast sailing, British-built, Copper bolted BARQUE

VITTORIA,

650 Tons Burthen,

Mosey Simpson, Commander,

LYING AT MALPUS, IN TRURO RIVER,

Has very superior accommodation for Steerage and Cabin Passengers.

The Commander having been many years in the North American Trade, can give much valuable information regarding the Colonies, to any that may feel disposed to take a passage in the said ship.

Apply to the CAPTAIN on board,

Mrs. SIMPSON, at the Seven Stars Inn, Truro,

Or to the Owner, NICHOLAS MITCHELL, Malpus.

Dated, February 13th, 1841.

E. HEARD, PRINTER, BOOKBINDER, &c., BOSCAWEN-STREET, TRURO.

agent had 600 applications in a fortnight, and the same year 3,690 men sailed from Plymouth for Australia, and 1,000 more for Quebec, bound for various parts of the Continent. Rich finds of copper were the attraction at this time, but in 1851 the Australian gold rush brought many more Cornishmen, for instance from St Just to the Bendigo area, seventy-two days of sailing, then inland to search the alluvials. Some had their hopes fulfilled: a story in the *West Briton*, of February 2nd, 1853 reports, 'A Cornishman, William Chenoweth, writes to his brother, in the neighbourhood of Camelford, from the diggings. He says, " . . . I left here [Willunga, 21 miles south of Adelaide] with [4 others from West Cornwall] . . . We worked very hard for the first seven weeks, and made about $1\frac{1}{2}$ oz of gold each; the other three weeks and four days we made about £4,500, making it £900 each. . . . in about two months I intend going again . . . I intend to lay my money out in land, as there will be a maintenance for my family . . . shoemakers are making fortunes here." ' That sum would be worth about thirty-five times as much today. Will Chenoweth was not the only man to see a greater future on the land rather than under it, and there was a steady farming settlement. Gold, however, was always a magic lure, and the two largest nuggets found in the Victoria goldfields fell to the Cornish. The Welcome nugget, weighing 185lb (84 kg), found at Ballarat in 1859 was shared by twenty-two Cousin Jacks, and the Welcome Stranger discovered in 1869 at Moliagul, 50 km west of Bendigo, the largest nugget ever found in the world, over 200lb (90.75kg) and worth £9,500 then, £304,000 - £323,000 now, by Richard Oates and John Deason of St Just and Scilly. Other Cornish adventurers turned to auxiliary businesses, from crushing mills to stores, to serve the steady flow of immigrants, 10,000 from Cornwall alone in 1875, in the second gold rush.

The *West Briton* of April 6th, 1832 said: 'The rage for

emigration that now prevails in the north of this county is wholly unprecedented in Cornwall; in different parishes from 200 to 300 persons each, have either departed or are preparing to depart to leave for Canada or the United States.' Many of these must have hoped to settle on the land for few American mining prospects were obvious yet, and north Cornwall is not mining country. For the copper miner the Keweenaw peninsula on the south coast of Lake Superior in the state of Michigan was the first great draw. Already being exploited by 1844, with twenty Cornishmen there, the 1850s saw a rush for copper not unlike the Californian gold rush, and more again in the 1860s. Thousands of Cornish came to an area reminiscent of Cornwall, to Copper Harbour, the richest copper country in its time, or to the Quincey Mine. Rowe says that in the 1870s 'there were more Cornishmen working at Calumet and Hecla mines in Michigan than there were at any other copper mine in the world.' Later some were to move away to Detroit or the great iron mountains

Moonta mining camp, South Australia, 1897

of Menominee and Gogebic. At the south west corner of Wisconsin, just into Illinois, was an area of rich lead ores, settled between 1830 and 1860 first by Americans, then Cornish miners, but by 1860 more than half the farmers there were Cornish.

Meantime, on the other side of the continent, gold had been found in California and the gold rush of 1849 was calling in more Cornish, some from home, some even from Australia. Today there are probably more Cornish in California than in any other state of the Union. Grass Valley and Nevada City, in the most profitable mining area, were predominantly Cornish. As in Australia many who made their pile moved to other states to become farmers. An interesting entry in the *West Briton* of August 30th, 1850 reported: 'A company has been formed in Breage for the purpose of sending parties to the gold diggings of California . . . eight men who are going out have been provided with tents and working tools . . . This is the first company of the kind . . . in Cornwall.' One wonders if any of them were as lucky as the Thomas brothers: 'Two miners, Nicholas and William Thomas, of the parish of Northhill, have lately returned to their homes from California. They left three years since last April . . . they continued to labour for above two years – the two returned . . . bringing with them above £1,500 each [£50-60,000 today]. Nicholas was a married man with three children, and when he left his family were pennyless and destitute, but the wife by industry at her needle, with the help of some good friends, has supported herself and family decently . . . ' *West Briton*, January 2nd, 1852.

As more and more settlers moved west the treasures of the mountain states began to be found, gold first in 1849 by a young Cornish Mormon, William Prouse, in the Carson Valley of western Nevada. This led to the discovery of the fabulous Comstock lode of gold and silver. Here again Cornish expertise was needed, and at a time of severe mining decline at home. It was recorded in the *West Briton* of August 12th, 1869 that Camborne men in California and Nevada were sending home to their families and relatives between £15,000 and £18,000 in the year, a sum equal to the combined wage bill of a score of mines in the Camborne district at that time. An early and rapid transition from placer-digging to lode mining, particularly in the second half of the century, in Utah, Montana, Idaho, Oregon, Washington and Dakota put Cornish experience at a premium, and the phone books of these states show how many Cornish came and stayed, though often in conflict with Irish immigrants. There was a gold rush to Colorado in 1859, and silver mining from 1877, and more gold at Cripple's Creek in 1891. Here, too, lode mining was rapidly established. Arizona was the last state to develop, with finds of gold, silver and copper after 1874, and again many Cornish prospectors remain in the state today. At the opposite end of the continent very little seems to have been written of Cornish in the Klondyke gold rush of 1896.

In South Africa the Governor of Cape Colony, Lord Charles Somerset, introduced a policy in 1820 of settling farmers as a barrier to hold the frontier against African tribesmen. Some 4,000 people were recruited, of which a small Cornish party of eleven men and their families under Benjamin Osler of Falmouth sailed from Portsmouth in January 1820. A new town and capital of Bathurst was created, and the Cornish group settled twelve miles away at a site they called Pendennis. Crop failure and other difficulties increasing, some returned home and others moved elsewhere in the colony, very few remaining. Stephen Sawle Osler founded a line of descendants in Simonstown. The real Cornish settlement began in 1852 when full exploitation of Namaqualand copper began. A German, von Schlich, sent for Cornish miners and built the village of Concordia for them. Success brought other Cornish to nearby mines but it was not an inviting site for families. Many of the miners took common-law wives locally and there are many coloured people with Tre, Pol and Pen surnames in the area still.

With the discovery of the first diamond 'pipe' in July, 1871, later named the Kimberley mine, came a rush of diggers of every nationality, 50,000 by 1872. The many Cornish there came from other mining fields as well as from home, many enough for a Cornish dinner to be advertised in December 1889. 1871 brought a gold rush to the Transvaal,and Millwood, above the Knysna Lagoon, had a short-lived boom in 1876. A solid and lasting gold source was found in the Witwatersrand from 1885. All three drew in their contingents of Cornish, many to move on later to other fields of South African life, where their descendants still thrive.

New Zealand, settled from the mid-nineteenth century, was almost totally agricultural, and remains so. There, and in every area where Cornish have settled, they have made their mark in as wide a range of social service and achievement as any community could wish for; often, it appears, flourishing in their new homes when remaining in Cornwall would have stifled and wasted their talents. In the preface to this book the loss to Cornwall by emigration of its able manpower was mentioned, though it must not be forgotten that poverty equally wastes abilities. The *West Briton* of February 1st, 1867 reported: 'The various committees appointed to carry out the extensive system of relief to the poor now organized at Redruth, have for the last fourteen days been unceasing in their labour . . . 670 bread and soup tickets were presented to as many half-starved men and women . . . ' And the *Royal Cornwall Gazette* in January 1868 said 'eight thousand miners have recently left Cornwall in search of bread.' Naturally, those who could went overseas, but how many? Bernard Deacon gives these figures, based on Registrar General's Reports, British Parliamentary Papers and Census Reports:

1841-50	net emigration	31,650
1851-60		35,464
1861-70		53,827
1871-80		65,560
1881-90		39,140
		225,641

and adds ' . . . in the 1890s emigration, particularly to the Rand . . . perhaps another 30,000 left Cornwall . . . gives an emigration total of up to 318,000 in the period 1841-1901, almost the same as the resident population in the latter year, i.e. 322,000.'

CHAPTER 16

The Arts and Sciences

Lives of great men all remind us
We can make our lives sublime,
And, departing, leave behind us
Footsteps in the sands of time.
H.W. Longfellow

CORNWALL has raised as great a quota as any part of Britain of fine minds and ingenious talents, though many have flourished beyond its borders, the centres of learning and patrons being best found in larger cities. To give any depth of biographical detail to the throng of achievers from the Duchy would stretch this note from pages to a whole library, and as the intent of this book is to describe mainly the life-style of ordinary people in their daily work these comments must be brief. Some of the biographies of the renowned progeny of the far west are noted below in the bibliography.

In the arts sculpture is restricted almost to one man, Nevil Northey Burnard (1818-1878), self-taught first and later by the leading Victorian sculptor Chantry, and much of his work was done in London. An early piece, a head of Wesley, can be seen on a building in his birthplace, the remote moorland village of Altarnun. High on a column at the top of Lemon Street in Truro is a standing figure of the explorer Richard Lander, one of his finer works. Sculpture apart, it is worth noting some of the fine detail that local stonemasons applied to granite buildings of the eighteenth and nineteenth centuries, work that is unlikely to be repeated, and also the well-proportioned lettering and design of many eighteenth century headstones.

The eccentric ex-bookseller Charles Fox (1749-1809) of Falmouth was a skilled portrait and landscape painter, and recorder of his travels around the Baltic, but his talents were known largely to his family and friends. A near contemporary, Henry Bone (1755-1834) of Truro was an apprentice to William Cookworthy, for whom he decorated Bristol porcelain. Moving to London as a watch enameller, he turned to miniature painting on ivory and enamel, eventually under the patronage of the Prince of Wales. He made some painting tours in Cornwall, but was principally an enameller of wide repute. John Opie (1761-1807) was the son of a mine carpenter of Blowinghouse near St Agnes, a talented artist from his youth. Noticed by Dr Wolcot (who had also helped Bone) he was introduced to patrons in London and the Court. Soon known as the 'Cornish Wonder' and elected to the Royal Academy where he showed 143 pictures of his prolific output. He was a busy illustrator and Professor of Painting, dying, it was said, from overwork. The County Museum at Truro has nineteen of his paintings.

There were many local artists of local interest throughout the century but the great flourishing of painting in the county came late in the century. Like J.M.W. Turner who made a sketching tour of the far west in 1811, Walter Langley (1852-1922) and Edwin Harris (1855-1906) visited Newlyn in 1882, and settled to paint. They were soon joined by other artists keen to follow the French style of outdoor painting, and the 'Newlyn School' of now highly regarded painters was founded, including Penzance-born Harold Harvey (1874-1941). J.M. Whistler (1834-1903) and Walter Sickert (1860-1942) came to St Ives in 1884 in the same way, and their enthusiasm brought others like Julius Olsson (1864-1942) to form the 'St Ives School'. Outside the 'schools' were marine painters like Henry Moore (1831-1895) and Henry

To the
Memory
OF
Capt. Richard Curgenven,
of the Royal Navy,
Who died August 30th, 1784,
Aged 47.

Rich'd Ofman.

Capt. Curgenven's slate memorial

Tuke (1858-1929) who preferred the big ships of Falmouth to fishing boats, but all these talented artists were incomers whose great gift to the county was the intimate view of everyday life and work they have left us.

One local impact made by the settlers came from the Arts and Crafts movement of Ruskin and Morris. Seasonal unemployment in the Newlyn fishery led J.D. Mackenzie and other artists to establish an Industrial Class in 1890 making beaten copper work and decorative enamels which were fashionably popular well into the new century. Examples of this work are the Earth, Air, Fire and Water panels on the façade of Newlyn Art Gallery, the gift of Passmore Edwards, opened in 1895, the galleon weather vane on the Seamen's Mission in Newlyn, and the collection in the Royal Cornwall Museum.

Music comes naturally to the Cornish, both in organised and spontaneous choirs, and in brass bands, still a feature of life today. There was a Philharmonic Society in Truro as early as 1797, and Music Festivals, also in Truro, from the early nineteenth century. Musical groups, vocal or instrumental, were commonplace in all Cornish towns.

Charles Incledon (1763-1826) of St Keverne, called by George III 'The British National Singer', was well-known in Vauxhall Gardens, and for many years at Covent Garden. William Beale (1784-1854) of Landrake was a Westminster chorister and at the Chapel Royal, later organist to Trinity College, Cambridge, and a minor composer. Fanny Moody of Redruth (1866-1945), the 'Cornish Nightingale', became the star of the Carl Rosa Opera Company, and later, with her husband, principal singer in their own successful company until her early retirement.

Christmas carols, part of the popular church services of the fifteenth and sixteenth centuries, were banned during the Commonwealth. They had almost fallen out of use, except among the poor, until Davies Gilbert (see p. 197), writing of them as a thing of the past, published his collection of traditional carols in 1822. Their real revival had to wait until later in the century and Thomas Merritt (1863-1908) of Illogan, with only a few months tuition, became a teacher of music and organist, renowned for his many carols and a hundred other musical works.

Truro, Falmouth and Penzance all had theatres, the latter town's being over the stables of the Union Hotel in Chapel Street, and lesser towns used large buildings or open spaces to receive travelling companies as well as local talent. The census of 1841 recorded ten comedians resident in Falmouth, though that description did not have quite the same meaning as it does today; entertainers would be nearer. The great actor, playwright and satirist Samuel Foote of Truro (1720-1777) trained in law after leaving Oxford University, but took to the stage. He became owner of the New Theatre, Haymarket, but performed in many other London theatres, often in comic rôles and satires and occasionally in dramatic works. He appears not to have acted in his home county.

Writers have been abundant in Cornwall, both native and English, making it remarkably well documented in the past, with Richard Carew's *The Survey of Cornwall* (1602) setting a high standard. At present there is a wealth of descriptive material being offered, ranging from pisky and Arthurian fantasy to researched monographs and local guides. No incomer wishing to inform himself of the past or the present should find any great difficulty, nor is there any excuse for ill-informed damage to what should be our successors' inheritance.

Outstanding from his time was William Borlase (1695-1772), born at Pendeen Manor near St Just, educated at Oxford, and returning to become Vicar of Ludgvan in 1722. His *Antiquities of Cornwall*, 1754, and *Natural History of Cornwall*, 1758, are monumental works, and yet only part of the wide-ranging

observations, correspondence and reports on the natural occur-
rences and social topics he made from a remote parish at the far
end of Britain.

Other outstanding historians were Thomas Tonkin (1678-
1742) and Richard Polwhele (1760-1838) whose works are still
valuable sources, and Samuel Drew (1765-1833), though the
latter was mainly a metaphysical writer, and later manager of
the Caxton Press. Francis Vyvyan Jago (later named Arundell)
(1780-1846), antiquarian and traveller, collected material for a
Cornish history which was later used by the Lysons in their
outstanding history. (Daniel L. 1762-1834; Samuel L. 1763-
1819).

John Wallis of Bodmin (1789-1866), statistician, collected a
wealth of information on the county.

Another great traveller was James Silk Buckingham of
Flushing (1786-1855) who founded the *Calcutta Journal* and later
the *Athenaeum*, while later at home building a reputation for his
humanitarian campaigns. Travelling less widely, in France and
England only, was Cyrus Redding of Penryn (1785-1870), a
journalist in Plymouth and London, wine expert and author of
An Itinerary of Cornwall which still makes interesting reading.
The West Penwith guides of Dr John A. Paris of 1815 and J.S.
Courtney of 1845 must also be noted.

Among the multitudes of seamen raised in the county some of
wider repute can be noted. There are the admirals Edward
'Dreadnought' Boscawen (1711-1761) of Tregothnan, on the Fal
north-east of Truro, MP for Truro and later Saltash, and Charles
Penrose (1759-1830) of St Gluvias near Penryn, both of whom
had lively and stirring careers. Sir Edward Pellew of Sparnon,
Breage, who destroyed the power of the Algerine pirates in
1816, the last to plague the Cornish coasts, also deserves mention. Two great navigators, William Bligh (1754-1817) of St
Tudy near Wadebridge, of the *Bounty* and later a Fellow of the

Royal Society, and Samuel Wallis (1728-1795) of Tremaine, Lanteglos-by-Camelford, circumnavigator and discoverer of Easter Island, helped to define the known world. Richard Lander (1804-1834) and his brother John (1807-1839) of Truro explored the little-known River Niger, and their exploits are remembered by a statue-crowned column looking down on the old city.

John Passmore Edwards of Blackwater near Truro (1823-1911) turned to journalism and newspaper ownership, including the progressive *Echo* and a number more. Always a reformer, he was very successful in business and the fortune he amassed was spent in founding seventy free libraries, many in Cornwall, hospitals, the Truro Technical School, and much more. One more journalist, noted also for his short stories, was H.D. Lowry of Truro (1869-1906) who worked on the *Pall Mall Gazette* and the *Morning Post*. An earlier reformer of a different kind and a different fate was William Lovett (1800-1877). Raised in Newlyn and trained as a carpenter, he moved to London in 1821 and was a prime mover in founding the London Working Men's Association (1836), and in drawing up the People's Charter (1838). His moderation split him from other Chartist leaders, but he continued to fight for the right of working men to a vote and to education. He died in poverty.

At the other end of the social scale were Sir W. Molesworth and Charles Buller (1806-48) of Polvellan, near Liskeard, MP for West Looe 1830-32 and 1832-48, a radical Liberal and collaborator with Molesworth. Sir William Molesworth (1810-55) of Pencarrow, near Bodmin, was a 'Philosophical Radical', MP for East Cornwall 1832-36, for Leeds 1837-41, and Southwark 1845-55, holding ministerial posts in the last. He was co-founder of the *London and Westminster Review* and the Reform Club. He advocated secret and household ballot with no religious discrimination, free trade, national education, better government

for Ireland, self-government for the colonies with no transportation and reform of the House of Lords. He was sponsor
and substantial financier of the Bodmin-Wadebridge Railway,
with its branch to Wenford Bridge, opened in 1834.

Caroline Fox of Falmouth (1819-1871) and her brother Barclay
(1817-1855), the diarists, must not be forgotten, for their meetings with many of the great figures of their time are recorded
with keen eyes. Better known, locally and nationally, were
Silas (1850-1935) and Joseph (1855-1937) Hocking, both prolific
fiction writers, Joseph with a strong Methodist bent, and Silas
more popular and reputed to have sold at least a million copies
of his books. Hocking's home, Penmare at Copperhouse, is now
a hotel. Greatly popular too, well into this century and still
reprinted, was Arthur Quiller-Couch of Bodmin (1863-1944), a
writer of style and distinction. He was for long a well-liked
Professor of English Literature at Cambridge, and a strong
supporter of everything Cornish and of Cornish writers.

The village versifiers must be remembered, less for the quality
of their works than for the insight their rhymes give into the
lives of the very poor, and their religious feelings. Penwith has
Henry Quick of Zennor (1792-1857) and his contemporaries,
Richard Williams of Sennen, Billy Foss of Sancreed, and Robert
Maybee of Scilly. A search for the writings of similar working,
or poverty stricken, labouring men in any Cornish town might
well be rewarding, for there were many such forgotten observers
of their times.

The sciences, apart from engineering, have also been well
represented in the county. Borlase has been mentioned, and
Humphry Davy (1778-1829), also from Ludgvan, had the same
wide-ranging curiosity. His interest in chemical science was
noticed by Davies Gilbert who set him on his career, culmina-
ting as Chemistry Professor at the Royal Institution, Michael
Faraday as his assistant, and President of the Royal Society. He

discovered the use of nitrous oxide as an anaesthetic, and in electrical experiments in 1807-8 isolated the elements potassium, sodium, calcium, barium, magnesium and strontium, adding to another new element, titanium, 'manaccanite', discovered in 1790 by the amateur geologist the Rev William Gregor (1761-1817) when holidaying with the Rev Richard Polwhele, q.v., at Manaccan. Davy's miners' safety lamp is everyday knowledge, but his reputation as a fine poet is far less well known, or his application of chemistry to agriculture, or his part in the foundation of the Zoological Society. His patron Davies (Giddy) Gilbert (1767-1839) of St Erth was a geologist and botanist and MP for Bodmin. Gilbert did much to help Trevithick and, like Davy, became President of the Royal Society. As an antiquary he was outstanding, publishing a fine *Parochial History of Cornwall*, and the first modern collection of traditional carols.

Joseph Carne (1782-1858) of Penzance managed the Cornwall Copper Company's works at Ventonleague, Hayle, and became an authority on Cornish geology in his time. He was elected Fellow of the Royal Society, and his mineral collection became the nucleus of the geological museum of the Royal Cornwall Geological Society at Penzance. Philip Rashleigh (1729-1811), author of two books on British minerals, amassed a remarkable collection, much of which is now in the Royal Cornwall Museum in Truro. William Pengelly (1812-1894) of Looe started life as a seaman but turned to schoolmastering and geology. He was made a Fellow of the Geographical Society and FRS, working mostly in Devon, where his exploration of Kent's Cavern, Torquay, became a landmark of prehistory.

Jonathan Couch (1789-1870) of Polperro trained at Guy's Hospital and became the doctor to his village for the rest of his life. He compiled *A History of British Fishes*, a *Cornish Fauna* and *A History of Polperro*, the first having a wide reputation. His co-eval Robert Were Fox, FRS, (1789-1877) of Falmouth, father of Caroline, q.v., noted the rate of increase of temperature in deep mines, and assisted Trevithick in the use of high-pressure steam. Another Cornish doctor, William Adams (1783-1827) of Morwenstowe was an outstanding specialist in eye diseases, opening his own hospital in London. He was knighted for his work. Also among doctors of repute is William Oliver (1695-1764) of Lower Tremenheere, near Ludgvan, who practised in Bath and whose place and name are still linked together. More humbly, perhaps, it was Andrew Pears, a barber of Mevagissey, whose invention in the 1790s of a pure and gentle soap added measurably to the cleanliness and health of nineteenth century England.

Finally, I must mention John Couch Adams (1819-1892), son of a farmer of Laneast, and one of the great scientists of his time. A natural mathematician, he computed the position of Neptune. He was an FRS among many other honours, Professor of Astronomy at Cambridge and could have been Astronomer Royal, which he refused, as he did a knighthood.

These are a few people, very often of humble origin, from a long roll of honour to which many more could be added from the period. It is a list still open and increasing. These creators of the Cornish heritage should be an inspiration for the future.

Postscript

LOOKING back from the 1890s to the 1790s we are surveying great changes in the lifestyle of Western man, moving a sophisticated agricultural society into a primitive industrial, technological and increasingly urban one. The divorce of people from their natural roots and the essential interdependence of living things was becoming endemic. The whole world was at last in view, though the impact of the West on other civilizations was still limited, and destructive of primitive societies only in restricted areas, particularly in the Americas, Australia and Africa.

The dynamism of industrialists and entrepreneurs, added to the exploding populations of western nations, moved millions into settlement of the continents beyond Europe, changing their nature and development with a speed that led too often to near genocide. No other life-form has dominated the world in this way before, and the problems created increase in complexity and difficulty of solution with each new generation.

Our century following has continued that course with increasing acceleration of population and technology, to create more and greater change than in any past period of human history. With it has often come a calamitous intrusion into the lives of every surviving primitive people, with debatable advantage, decline or extinction. The creature life of the world has been exploited, diminished or destroyed, threatening a biological disaster.

Now, near the end of the century, the benefits of the technological revolution are also proving less than ideal. So much has the slow course of evolution been speeded up, the buried

185

remains of past life exposed for burning, and new substances created without complete understanding, that the very future of the world is being brought into question. Man's intelligence is now facing the supreme test: whether it can be applied to create a viable long-term successful future for the human race in an economy in harmony with its environment, or not. That intelligence, constructive and destructive, cannot be underrated. Its achievements have been prodigious, and its limits yet unexplored; there can be better to come.

Bibliography

THE sources and references used have not been noted in the text, partly to avoid clutter on the page, but mostly because, in this well-documented county, several sources have been compared before shaping the conclusion. My grateful thanks are offered to the authors whose writings I have used, and I trust I have always acknowledged my debt in this list.

CA   —   Cornish Archaeology
JRIC   —   Journal of the Royal Institution of Cornwall
JTS   —   Journal of the Trevithick Society
BRCPS —   Reports of the Royal Cornwall Polytechnic Society
TSNL   —   Trevithick Society News Letter

Adburgham, A. *A Radical Aristocrat*, Tabb House, Padstow, 1990

Allen, J. *History of the Borough of Liskeard*, 1856

ALS Research Group, Min. of Ag. and Fish. *History of Agriculture and Land Use in the Land's End Peninsula*, 1952

Andrews, C.T. *The First Cornish Hospital*, Truro, 1975

Anthony, C.H. *Hayle, W. Cornwall and Helston Railways*, Oakwood Press, 1968

Axford, E.C. *Bodmin Moor*, David & Charles, Newton Abbot, 1975

Barton, D.B. *The Redruth & Chasewater Railway*, Barton, Truro, 1960

Barton, D.B. *The Cornish Beam Engine*, Barton, Truro, 1965

Barton, D.B. *A History of Tin Mining and Smelting in Cornwall*, Barton, Truro, 1967

Barton, D.B. *A History of Copper Mining in Cornwall and Devon*, Barton, Truro, 1968

Barton, D.B. *Essays in Cornish Mining History*, vols. 1 & 2, Barton, Truro, 1968, 1970

Barton, R.M. *An Introduction to the Geology of Cornwall*, Barton, Truro, 1964

Barton, R.M. *A History of the Cornish China Clay Industry*, Barton, Truro, 1966

Barton, R.M. ed. *Life in Cornwall*, 4 vols. 1810-1899, Barton, Truro, 1970-4

Beckett, R. *A Pictorial Booklet for the Tercentenary of Falmouth*, 1962

Benney, D.E. *Cornish Watermills*, Barton, Truro, 1972

Berriman, H. *Art and Crafts in Newlyn 1890-1930*, Newlyn Orion Gallery, 1986

Blight, J.T. *A Week at the Land's End (1861)*, facsimile, Alison Hodge, Penzance, 1989

Bliss, V. *History of Hayle*, Penwith Dist. Council, 1978

Boase, G.C. *Collectanea Cornubiensis*, 1900

Borlase, W. *Antiquities of the County of Cornwall*, Oxford, 1754

Borlase, W. *The Natural History of Cornwall*, Oxford, 1758

Borlase, W.C. *Sea Sands on Soils in Cornwall*, JRIC, 1878-1879

Bosanketh, E. *Tin (1888)*, repr. J. Brooke, 1988

Brown, H.M. *Cornish Clocks and Clockmakers*, David and Charles, Newton Abbot, 1961 & 1970

Brunton, A. *Bodmin Gaol*, Orchard Publications, Chudleigh, 1992

Buller, J. *St Just in Penwith*, Rodda, Penzance 1842, facs. Dyllansow Truran, Redruth, 1983

Burt, R. *John Taylor, Mining Entrepreneur & Engineer, 1779-1863*, Moorland Publishing Co., Buxton, 1977

Carew, R. *Survey of Cornwall, 1602*, see Halliday

Carter, C. *The Blizzard of '91*, 1971

Chepstow Society *Brunel's Tubular Suspension Bridge over the River Wye*, 1856, repr. Chepstow, 1976

Cheshire, V.M. & F.J. *The Cornishman's House*, Barton, 1968

Christopher, G.P. *Story of Hain Steamship Co. – See Breezes*, no. 41, vol. VII, p.274, May, 1949

Clarke, E.D. *Tour Through the South of England*, London, 1796

Collins, J.H. *The West of England Mining District*. 1897.

Collins, W. *Rambles Beyond Railways*, 1851, later reprs.

Corin, J. *Fishermen's Conflict*, Tops'l Books, 1988

Corin, J. *Levant, A Champion Cornish Mine*, Trevithick Soc., 1992

Couch, J. *Pilchard Trade*, RRCPS, 1835

Couch, J. RRCPS. 1840

Courtney, J.S. RRCPS, p.81 ff. 1838

Courtney, J.S. *Penzance Poor Law Union*, RRCPS, 1842

Courtney, J.S. *Guide to Penzance and Its Neighbourhood*, Penzance, 1845

Davison, E.H. *Handbook of Cornish Geology*, Blackford, Truro, 1930

Deacon, B. *Liskeard and Its People*, priv. pub. 1989

Dines, H.G. *The Metalliferous Mining District of S.W. England*, HMSO, 1956

Douch, H.L. *Cornish Windmills*, Blackford, Truro, 1963

Douch, H.L. *Old Cornish Inns*, Barton, Truro, 1966

Drew, J.H. *Rail and Sail to Pentewan*, Twelveheads Press, Truro, 1986

Drew, S. *A History of Cornwall, vol. 2*. 1790.

Earl, B. *Cornish Mining*, Barton, Truro, 1968

Earl, B. *Kennal Vale Explosive Works*, TSNL no. 6, 1974

Earl, B. *Perranporth Explosive Works*, TSNL no. 14, 1976

Earl, B. *Cornish Explosives*, Trevithick Soc., 1978

Edmonds, McKeown & Williams *British Regional Geology, South West England*, HMSO, 1969

Evans, R.E. & Prettyman, G.W. *Pentewan*, St Austell, 1986

Fal History Group *History Round the Fal*, U. of Exeter, 1980

Farr, G. *West Country Passenger Steamers*, Tilling, 1956

Fiennes, C. *Journeys of C.F. (1698)*, Cresset Press, 1949

Fox, C. & Greenacre, F. *Newlyn School 1880-1900*, Newlyn Orion Gallery, 1979

Fox, H. *History and Statistics of Pilchard Fishery*, RRCPS, 1878

Fox, H. *Story of William Cookworthy*, Kingsbridge, 1972

Fox, H.S.A. *Outfield Cultivation in Devon and Cornwall*, (see Havinden, M.A.), 1973.

Fraser, R. *A General View of the County of Cornwall*, 1794

Fulton, R. *A Report on the Proposed Canal between the River Heyl and Helford*, 1796

Gay, S.E. *Old Falmouth*, London, 1903

Graham, F. *Smuggling in Cornwall*, N.J. Clarke, Lyme Regis, 1986

Guthrie, A. *Goldherring*, CA no. 6, 1969

Hadfield, C. *Canals of SW England*, David & Charles, Newton Abbot, 1969

Hain, E. *Prisoner of War in France*, Duckworth, 1914

Halliday, F.E. *Richard Carew of Antony*, Melrose, 1953

Hamilton Jenkin, A.K. *The Cornish Miner*, Allen & Unwin, 1927

Hamilton Jenkin, A.K. *Cornwall and Its People*, Dent, 1945 (later reprints)

Harris, H. & Ellis, M. *The Bude Canal*, David & Charles, 1972

Harris, J. *My Autobiography*, London, Falmouth, Penryn and Exeter, 1882

Harris, T.R. *Sir Goldsworthy Gurney*, Trevithick & Old Cornwall Societies, 1975

Hatchett, C. *A Tour Through the Counties of England and Wales in 1796*, ed. A. Raistrick, 1967

Harvey & Co. *Catalogue*, 1884, repro. Barton, Truro, 1973

Havinden, M.A. ed. Exeter Papers in Econ. Hist. no. 8, *Husbandry and Marketing in the SW*. 1973.

Hencken, H.O'N. *Archaeology of Cornwall and Scilly*, Methuen, 1932

Henderson, C. & Coates, H. *Old Cornish Bridges*, 1928, repr. Barton, Truro, 1972

Henwood, G. *Cornwall's Mines and Miners*, ed. R. Burt, Barton, Truro, 1972

Higgans, J. *Angarrack Smelting House*, MSS Cornwall County Library, JTS no. 7, p.37, 1979-80

Hippisley-Coxe, A.D. *Smuggling in the West Country 1700-1850*, Tabb House, Padstow, 1984

Hodge, J. *Illustrated Life of R. Trevithick*, Shire, 1973

Hollowood, B. *Cornish Engineers*, priv. pub. for Holman Brothers Ltd., 1951

Hopkinson, D. *Edward Penrose Arnold*, Alison Hodge, 1981

Hoskins, W.G. *One Man's England*, BBC, London, 1976

Hudson, W.H. *The Land's End*, Hutchinson, 1908, repr. Wildwood House, London, 1981

Jenkin, J. *History of the Old Delabole Slate Quarry*, Eveleigh, Launceston, 1888

Keast, J. *The Story of Fowey*, Townsend, Exeter, 1950

Keast, J. *History of East & West Looe*, Phillimore, 1987

Kendell, J. *Humphry Davy, 'Pilot' of Penzance*, 1954 & 59

Kittridge, A. *Passenger Steamers of the River Fal*, Twelveheads Press, Truro, 1988

Laws, P. *Gas Industry in Cornwall*, TSNL no. 8, 1975, no. 10, 1975, no. 12, 1976

Leeds, E.T. *Chun Castle, Archaeologia no. 76.*

Lemon, C. *Statistics of the Copper Mines of Cornwall*, J. of Statistical Soc. of London, 1838

Lemon, C. *Agricultural Products of Cornwall, British Association Reports*, 1841

Lewis, G.R. *The Stannaries*, repr. Barton, Truro, 1965

Lewis, M.J.T. *The Pentewan Railway*, Twelveheads Press, Truro, 1960

Lysons, D. & S. *Magna Britannia, vol. 3*, Cornwall, 1814

Maclean, J. *Parochial & Family History of the Deanery of Trigg Minor*, 1868

McGrady, R. *Music and Musicians in Early Nineteenth Century Cornwall*, U. of Exeter Press, 1991

Marshall, W. *Rural Economy of the W. of England*, London, 1796

Matthews, J.H. *History of St Ives, Lelant and Towednack*, Elliot Stock, London, 1892

Maxwell, I.S. *Farming in Cornwall ca. 1800*, RRCPS, 1942

Maxwell, I.S. *Historical Atlas of W. Penwith*, U. of Sheffield, 1976

Messenger, M.J. *Caradon and Looe, the Canal, Railway and Mines*, Twelveheads Press, Truro, 1978

Minchinton, W.E., ed. Exeter Papers in Econ. Hist. no. 5, *Farming and Transport in the SW*, 1972

Minchinton, W.E. & Perkins, J. *Tidemills of Devon and Cornwall*, U. of Exeter, 1971

Mitchell, F.B. *Redruth Hospital, 1863-1981*, Camborne, 1981

Mitchell, S. *Early History of Hayle Foundry, 1770-1833*, ed. J. Hambley Rowe, undated

Moyle, R. *Wheat Harvesting*, Communications to the Board of Agriculture, vol. IV, 1805

Mumford, C. *Portrait of the Isles of Scilly*, Hale, London, 1967

Nance, R.M. *Pillas, an Extinct Grain*, Old Cornwall, vol. 1, no. 12

Noall, C. *History of Cornish Mail & Stage-coaches*, Barton, Truro, 1963

Noall, C. *Levant*, Barton, Truro, 1970

Noall, C. *Smuggling in Cornwall*, Barton, Truro, 1971

Noall, C. *Cornish Seines and Seiners*, Barton, Truro, 1972

Noall, C. *The Book of Hayle*, Barracuda, Buckingham, 1985

O'Donaghue & Appleyard *Hain of St Ives*, World Ship Soc., Kendal, 1986

Oliver, A.S. *Boats and Boatbuilding in W. Cornwall*, Barton, Truro, 1971

Orchard, W.G. ed. *A Glossary of Mining Terms*, Dyllansow Truran, Redruth, 1991

Pascoe, W.H. *History of the Cornish Copper Company*, Dyllansow Truran, Redruth, undated

Paynter, S.W. *Old St Ives, Reminiscences of Wm. Paynter*, Lanham, St Ives, 1927

Pearce, J. *The Wesleys in Cornwall*, Barton, Truro, 1964

Pearce, R. *Ports and Harbours of Cornwall*, Warne, St Austell, 1963

Penderill-Church, J. *William Cookworthy*, Barton, 1972

Penhallurick, R. *Tin in Antiquity*, Institute of Metals, London, 1986

Philip, W. *Mineralogy*, London, 1887

Philp, J. (printer), *A Panorama of Falmouth*, *c.* 1827

Polwhele, R. *History of Cornwall*, Truro, 1803-8

Pool, P.A.S. *Place Names of W. Penwith*, Fed. of O. Corn. Socs., 1973

Pool, P.A.S. *History of Penzance*, Boro. of Pz., 1974

Pool, P.A.S. *Henry Quick of Zennor*, Truran, 1984

Pool, P.A.S. *William Borlase*, Roy. Inst. of Cornwall, 1986

Pounds, M.J.G. *Historical Geography of Cornwall*, MSS, RIC, 1942

Pounds, M.J.G. *Cornish Fish Cellars*, Antiquity, Vol. XVIII, 1944

Pryce, W. *Mineralogia Cornubiensis*, London, 1778

Pudney, J. *Brunel and His World*, Thames & Hudson, 1974

Reade, L. *The Branch Lines of Cornwall*, Atlantic Publrs., St Day, 1984

Redding, C. *Illust. Itinerary of the Cty. of Cornwall*, London, 1842

Roberts, G.E.P. *The Stannaries, Blowing Houses and Coinage Halls*, Trans. Corn. Inst. Engineers, NS vol. XI, 1955

Robson, J. & Nance, R.M. *Geological terms used in SW England*, Trans. Roy. Geol. Soc., vol. XIX, pt. 1, 1955-6

Roddis, R.J. *Cornish Harbours*, Johnson, London, 1957

Roddis, R.J. *Penryn*, Barton, Truro, 1964

Rowe, J. *Cornwall in the Age of the Industrial Revolution*, U. of Liverpool, 1953

Rowe, J., see Minchinton, paper 2, *Higher Farming in Cornwall*

Short, J.T. *Prisoners of War in France, 1804-1814*, Duckworth, 1914

Southey, R. *(Don Espriella) Letters from England*, 1802

Spreadbury, I.D. *Famous Men and Women of Cornish Birth*, Kingston, 1972

Stanier, P. *John Freeman and the Cornish Granite Industry*, JTS no. 13, 1986, p.7, no. 14, 1987, p.93

Stanier, P. *Cornwall's Literary Heritage*, Twelveheads Press, 1992

Stevens, J. *A Cornish Farmer's Diary*, ed. Pool, 1977

Stockdale, F.W.L. *Excursions Through Cornwall 1824*, Barton, Truro, 1972

Stratton, J.M. *Agricultural Records AD 220-1968*, London, 1969

Tangye, M. *Portreath*, priv. pub., 1968

Tate, W.E. *Enclosure Acts and Awards*, D & C Notes and Queries, vol. XXI

Thomas, D.& J. *Regional History of Railways of G.B., West Country*, Phoenix, 1960

Thomas, J. *Changes in Agriculture in Cornwall since 1800*, J. of Statistical Soc., vol. XXXII, 1869

Thomas, R. *History and Description of the Town and Harbour of Falmouth*, Trathan, Falmouth, 1828

Todd, A.C. & Laws, P. *Industrial Archaeology of Cornwall*, David & Charles, Newton Abbot, 1972

Tregellas, L.T. *Rural Population of Cornwall*, Netherton & Worth, Truro & London, 1879

Trethowan, D.M. *Porthleven, Its Commercial Growth & Decline, 1811-1958*, Exeter P's. in Econ. Hist. no. 4

Turner, J.T.F. *A Familiar Description of the Old Delabole Slate Quarry*, Lewis, Stonehouse, 1865

Vale, E. *The Harveys of Hayle*, Barton, Truro, 1966

Vivian, S. *The Story of the Vivians*, ch.x. priv.pub., 1989, 1990

Wailes, R. *A Source Book of Windmills and Watermills*, Ward Lock, 1979

Ward-Jackson, C.H. *Ships and Shipbuilders of a West Country Seaport, Fowey 1786-1939*, Twelveheads Pr., Truro, 1986

Warner, Rev. J. *A Tour Through Cornwall in the Autumn of 1808*, London, 1809

Watson, W.D. *Pillas, more about*, Old Cornwall vol. 2, no. 9

Whetter, J.C.A. *The History of Falmouth*, Dyllansow Truran, Redruth, 1981

Whetter, J.C.A. *Rise of the Port of Falmouth, 1600-1800*, Exeter Papers in Econ. Hist. no. 4

Williams, J.A. *Cornish Tokens*, Barton, Truro, undated

Williams Perran Foundry, *Catalogue*, ca. 1870, repr. Trevithick Society, Camborne, 1976

Woodfin, R.J. *The Cornwall Railway*, Barton, Truro, 1972

Worgan, G.B. *A General View of the Agriculture of the County of Cornwall*, London, 1811

Worth, R.H. *Dartmoor*, 1953, rep. & ed. Barton, Truro, 1967

Miscellaneous

Act of George III 1775, Mevagissey Harbour

Act of George III 1776, St Ives Pilchard Fishery

Act of George III 1793, 17th June, Trevaunance Pier Co.

Act of Victoria 1841, St Ives Pilchard Fishery

Account Book of St Ives Waywardens, 1833-1849

JTS, no. 13, 1986

JTS, no. 15, 1988

TSNL, no. 8, no. 63, p. 5, no. 72, p. 8

Proc. W. Corn. Field Club, vol. 2, no. 2, p. 29

Trans. Pz. Nat. Hist. & Antiqn. Soc., vol. 1, pilchards

Trans. Pz. Nat. Hist. & Antiqn. Soc., 1852, p. 60

Old Cornwall, vol. VII, no. 9, p. 411

Old Cornwall, vol. VII, no. 10, p. 444 and p. 466

Rep. of Ctte. to Survey Proposed Lines of Canal from Bude into the Interior of Cornwall & Devon, April 15th, 1818

Sand and Ancient Rights of Farmers, H.N. at Courtney Liby., RIC, Truro, p. 101 *Sea Sand and Sanding Ways*, D. & C. Notes & Queries, vol. XXII

The Complete Farmer, a General Dictionary, London, 1807

Selected Biographies or Notes

THE titles below should be available from the County Library or the Courtney Library at the Royal Cornwall Museum. The Cornish Studies Library, Redruth, is the prime source, but local branch libraries should be consulted first.

C.Ch.   =   *Cornish Characters*, S. Baring-Gould, London, 1909
C.W.   =   *Cornish Worthies, pts. I & II*, W.H. Tregellas,
            London, 1884
JRIC   =   *Journal of the Royal Institution of Cornwall*
JTS   =   *Journal of the Trevithick Society*
RCG   =   *Royal Cornwall Gazette*, Truro
RRCPS   =   Royal Cornwall Polytechnic Soc. Reports,
            Falmouth

Adams, John Couch, C.Ch. p. 83
Allen, Ralph, C.W. vol. I, p. 1. *Parentage and Ancestry of R.A.*,
    J.H. Rowe, JRIC, 52
Arnold, Edward Penrose, *A Victorian Family Portrait*, D.
    Hopkinson, A. Hodge, 1981
Austen, Joseph Thomas, see Treffry
Basset, Sir Francis, C.W. vol. I, p. 128 on.
Bickford, William, W.B. 'Inventor of the Miners' Safety Fuse',
    A.K. Hamilton Jenkin, pamphlet
Bligh, Capt.William, C.W. vol. I, p. 137. R. Humble, Barker,
    1976
Bolitho, family, Thomas B., smelter and banker, RCG, 15.1.1858,
    p. 5 col. 1, p. 8, col. 4 T. Bedford B. RRCPS 1923, p. 76
Bone, Henry, C.W. vol. I, p. 159 Borlase, William, C.W. vol. I,
    p. 167. P.A.S. Pool, Truro, 1986
Boscawen, Admiral Edward, C.W. vol. I, p. 189-237
Brunel, Isambard Kingdom, Life of, London, 1870, repr. 1971
    L.T.C. Rolt, London, 1957, repr. 1970
Buckingham, James Silk, Longmans, 2 vols, 1855. C.CH., p.
    455, R.E. Turner, Wms. & Norgate, 1934
Burnard, Nevil Northey, C.Ch. p. 186 *A Wayward Genius*, Mary
    Martin, Lodenek Press, 1978
Carne, Joseph, RCG, 15.10.1858, brief obit. p 8, col. 4
Carter, Capt. Harry *Autobiography of a Cornish Smuggler*, 1894,
    facsm. Barton, Truro, 1971, ditto, Tor Mk. 1991

Cookworthy, William, *The Story of W.C.*, H. Fox, C. Museum, Kingsbridge, 1972

Couch, Jonathan, *Life of J.C.*, John Philp, 1891

Davy, Humphry, C.W. vol. I, p. 245. *H.D. Poet and Philosopher*, T.E. Thorpe, 1896 *The Mercurial Chemist*, Anne Treneere, London 1963

Edwards, Passmore *J.P.E., Philanthropist*, Burrage P.E., R. Angove, *Cornish Life*, vol. 11, No. 5, May 1984

Foote, Samuel, C.W. vol. I, p. 311. C.Ch. p. 280

Fox, Barclay *The Journal of*, ed. R.L. Brett, Bell & Hyman, London, 1979

Fox, Caroline, Wilson Harris, Constable, 1944, Journals of C.F., ed. W. Monk, Elek, 1972

Fox, Robert Were *Life and Work of R.W.F.* (v. brief), L.A. Bauer, Terres. Mag & Atmos. Elect., Cincinatti, Dec. 1910

Gilbert, Davies, C.Ch. p. 675. *Beyond the Blaze*, A.C. Todd, Barton, 1967

Gurney, Sir Goldsworthy, RCG, 1.2.1884, p. 7, col. 4, C.Ch. p. 192. T.R. Harris, Trevithick Soc., 1975

Harris, John, C.Ch. p. 692

Harveys of Hayle, Edmund Vale, Barton, 1966

Hawkins, Sir Christopher, C.Ch. p. 515

Holman family, *Cornish Engineers*, B. Hollowood, private print for Holman Bros., Camborne, 1951

Hornblower family, JTS no. 4, 1976, p. 7, and no. 5, 1977, p. 67

Incledon, Michael, C.W. vol. II, p. 67

Lander, Richard & John, John Saunders, *Travels of . . . into the interior of Africa*, London, 1836. C.W. vol. II, p. 197

Lemon, Sir Charles, RRCPS, 1912, p. 75

Lovett, William, *Life and Struggle of W.L.*, Garland, 1984

Merritt, Thomas, *The Illogan Musicians*, W.G. Donnithorne

Moody, Fanny, *The Cornish Nightingale*, D. Bray, *Cornish Life*, vol. 5, no. 1, 1978, p. 18

Molesworth, Sir William, *A Radical Aristocrat*, A. Adburgham, Tabb House, Padstow, 1990

Murdoch, William, W.M., C.H. Rivers, Earle, Redruth, 1947 *Faithful Servant*, J.A. McCash, Charter. & Mech. *Engineer*, London, 1966

Opie, John, C.W. vol. II, p. 243. *J.O. & His Circle, Ada Earland, Hutchinson, 1911*

Pellew, Sir Edward, C.W. vol. I, p. 291

Pengelly, William, C.Ch. p. 1

Penrose, Admiral Charles, C.Ch. p. 500

Praed, William, Rev. Hawker, Devon Assoc. vol. 6, p. 278

Rashleigh, family, T.L. Honey, RRCPS, 1939, p. 26

Rashleigh, Jonathan, obit. RCG, 20.4.1905, p. 7, col. 2,3

Rashleigh, Philip, A. Russell, JRIC no. 89, p. 96

Smeaton, John, A.W. Skempton, T. Telford, London, 1981

Stevens, James, *A Cornish Farmer's Diary*, ed. & published P.A.S. Pool, 1977

Taylor, John & Co., *J.T. Mining Entrepreneur* etc., R. Burt, Moorland, 1977

Treffry, Joseph, *The Treffrys and Cornish Industry*, Penderill-Church, 198? typescript photocopy, Courtney Liby. *The King of Mid-Cornwall*, J. Keast, Dyllansow Truran, Redruth, 1982

Trengrouse, Henry, C.Ch. p. 59

Trevithick, Richard, C.W. vol. II, p. 305. *The Cornish Giant*, L.T.C. Rolt, Litterworth, 1960 *R.T. Engineer & Man*, H.W. Dickinson & A. Titley, Cambridge, 1934

Wesley, John & Charles, *The Wesleys in Cornwall*, J. Pearce, Barton, 1964

Williams family of Scorrier, see individual entries in *Collectanea Cornubiensis*, Boase, G.C., 1900

Woolf, Arthur, T.R. Harris, Barton, 1966

Some Sources for Cornish Emigration

Balkeman, A.A. *Cornish Immigrants to South Africa*, Cape Town, 1978

Berthoff, R.T. *British Immigrants in Industrial America*

Brook & Allbutt *Shropshire Lead Mines*, Moorland, 1973

Deacon, B. 'How Many Went? – Size of the great Cornish emigration of the 19th cent.', MSS 6/1986, Corn. Cty. Liby. C325.2/094237 Deacon B. 'Cornish Emigration' JRIC 1986/7, p.84

Faull, J. *The Cornish in Australia*, Maryborough

Harris, A. *Cumberland Iron, the story of Hodbarrow Mine 1855-1968*, Barton, Truro, 1970

Harris, T.R. *The Copper King(T. Williams of Llanidan)*, Liverpool Univ. Press, 1964

Hopkins, R. *Where Now Cousin Jack?* Aust. Bicentennial Auth., Ballarat, 1988

Jewell, J. *Cornish in America, Linden, Wisconsin*, Cornish Miner Press, Linden, 1990

Kirkham, N. *Derbyshire Lead Mining*, Barton, Truro, 1868

Payton, P. *The Cornish Farmer in Australia*, Redruth, 1987

Payton, P. *The Cornish Miner in Australia*, Redruth

Raistrick & Jennings *A History of Lead Mining in the Pennines*, Longmans, 1965

Rowe, J. *The Hard Rock Men, Cornish Immigrants and the North American Mining Frontier*, Liverpool U.P., 1974

Rowse, A.L. *The Cornish in America*, Macmillan, 1969

Short, C.C. *Migration, Methodism & Mining in the North*, JTS no. 18, p.2, 1991

Todd, A.C. *The Cornish Miner in America*, Barton, Truro, 1967

Todd, A.C. *The Search for Silver, Cornish Miners in Mexico 1824-1947*, Lodenek Press, Padstow, 1977

Todd & James *Ever Westward the Land*, U. of Exeter P. 1986

Trescatheric, B. *Roose, A Cornish Village in Furness*, Hougenai Press, Barrow-in-Furness, 1983

APPENDIX

Some Weights and Measures

EXACT equivalents are not always reliable; these are taken from the best sources available.

Cornish miles tend to be variable.

Cornish acre	= 1.82 larger than English
1 sack of flour	= $2\frac{1}{2}$ bushels = 140 lb
1 bushel of flour	= 56 lb
1 Cornish bushel	= 3 Winchester corn bushels
1 Winchester bushel	= 8 gallons, 80 lb
1 quartern loaf	= 4 lb 5 oz $8\frac{1}{2}$ drams
1 bushel of coal	= 77 lb or 84 lb in engine tests, or 94 lb acc. to Hamilton Jenkin
1 chaldron	= 36 Winchester bushels
1 chaldron of coal	= $25\frac{1}{2}$ cwt 2,856 lb 1,295.5 kg
1 way	= 72 bushels at Portreath and Hayle, 64 elsewhere
1 hogshead	= 54 gallons, 63 wine gallons, 3,000 pilchards
6 imperial gallons	= 7 wine gallons
1 anker	= $8\frac{1}{2}$ imperial gallons
1 last of fish	= 10,000 fish
1 pack of charcoal	= 60 imperial gallons, 3 bushels
A kibble, various sizes	= maximum 12 cwt = 610 kg
A pare of men	= 2 men & 4 boys, average
A pare of pack mules	As required, up to 70 +

Index